"There is no one who knows more about the f... credibly illustrate the rewards of entrepreneurship—than Elaine ... *The Million-Dollar, One-Person Business* is a useful and inspiring guide to every would-be self-starter."

—**TOM POST**, former managing editor of *Forbes* and coauthor of *Unleashing the Innovators*

"Running a high-revenue one-person business isn't just about the money— it's about gaining the freedom to live your life in a way that matters to you and to give back to others in meaningful ways. In *The Million-Dollar, One-Person Business*, author and veteran small-business journalist Elaine Pofeldt draws on the stories and strategies of real entrepreneurs to create a highly readable and instructive roadmap for achieving these goals."

—**ANNE FIELD**, journalist and author of the *Forbes* blog *Not Only for Profit*

"Free agents have unprecedented opportunities to earn a great living and create the lifestyle they really want. *The Million-Dollar, One-Person Business* unlocks strategies that will help solo entrepreneurs achieve more than they ever thought possible."

—**MATT BARRIE**, CEO of Freelancer.com

"*The Million-Dollar, One-Person Business* is proof that you can have the life and career you desire if you dare to dream big."

—**SASAN GOODARZI**, executive vice president and general manager of Intuit Small Business

"Traditional, hierarchical careers are no longer the best path for many. Breaking free is incredibly empowering and can exponentially increase earnings for savvy professionals. This book is an excellent source of guidance for people carving new paths to help them through the many choices they face."

—**STEPHANE KASRIEL**, CEO of Upwork

"Pofeldt's book is the first stop for any entrepreneur who wants to make a real go of it."

—**HANK GILMAN**, owner and editor of High Water Press and former deputy editor of *Fortune* magazine

THE
MILLION-DOLLAR,
ONE-PERSON
BUSINESS

THE

MILLION-DOLLAR,

ONE-PERSON

BUSINESS

MAKE GREAT MONEY. WORK THE WAY YOU LIKE.
HAVE THE LIFE YOU WANT.

ELAINE POFELDT

LORENA JONES BOOKS
California | New York

Library of Congress Cataloging-in-Publication Data
is on file with the publisher.

Hardcover ISBN: 978-0-399-57896-0
eBook ISBN: 978-0-399-57897-7

Printed in the United States

Design by Lizzie Allen

10 9 8 7 6 5 4 3 2 1

First Edition

To my husband, Bob, for your love, support, and encouragement through all we have experienced together.

To my children, Anna, Emily, Sarah, and Robert for constantly inspiring me with your energy, enthusiasm, curiosity, and joyfulness.

And to my parents, Francine and Walter, for never discouraging me from pursuing the impractical career of writing.

CONTENTS

FOREWORD

By Verne Harnish, Founder,
Entrepreneurs' Organization

Running a business is ultimately about freedom and independence —
and there has never been a better time to go after that dream.
New technologies have made it easier and more affordable to start
a business than ever before. In a global marketplace, even tiny,
home-based businesses can reach a vast, international audience
of customers.

The challenge for many small business owners is scaling their
revenues and profits in an ultra-lean operation. The vast majority
of small businesses in the United States are one-person firms. In
many cases, the owners struggle to build a sustainable business that
can support them and their families. They don't have anything left
over to invest in growth. That is because of a knowledge gap. Many
owners have never learned how to create a high-revenue, high-
profit business without adding a lot of overhead. It's not something
you'll learn in school or even from other business owners.

The Million-Dollar, One-Person Business closes that gap. It offers a road map to creating a seven-figure, ultra-lean firm by sharing the strategies of entrepreneurs who have approached and hit $1 million in revenue before adding employees. From their experiences, you'll learn how to come up with the right business idea, how to develop concrete strategies you can use to turn your vision into reality, and how to scale your revenues and profits once they start rolling in.

Once you know how to create a million-dollar, one-person business, you'll have many possibilities in front of you. Some owners choose to keep their businesses small, building them around a lifestyle they love. Others decide to follow the path outlined in my book, *Scaling Up* (Rockefeller Habits 2.0), and create fast-growing, job-creating firms. No matter which route you choose, you'll have exciting options.

ACKNOWLEDGMENTS

Writing a book requires a great team, and I am grateful for the many individuals who contributed to *The Million-Dollar, One-Person Business*.

This book would never have been written without my dear friend, environmentalist Byron Kennard, who encouraged me to put the words on paper, week after week.

I am grateful to my agent, Leila Campoli, for seeing the potential for this idea and making it possible to bring it to a wide audience. Thank you, also, to my editor, Lorena Jones, for believing in the book and for your great insights in editing it, and to copyeditor Kristi Hein for the many smart and subtle improvements you made. I also owe gratitude to Ten Speed designer Lizzie Allen, production manager Heather Porter, and marketer and publicist Daniel Wikey.

Thank you to every entrepreneur who shared stories with me for this book and to the experts who contributed their knowledge.

Thank you to Sol Orwell for helping me connect with many of the million-dollar entrepreneurs I have profiled.

I'd like to thank editors Xana Antunes, Glenn Coleman, Susan Crandell, Diane Harris, Loren Feldman, Yasmin Ghahremani, Lori Ioannou, Scott Medintz, Peggy Northrop, and Tom Post for giving me many opportunities to explore the potential of the one-person business in my journalism. I'd also like to express my appreciation to Verne Harnish for showing me, in many ways, how entrepreneurship can pave a path to freedom.

Writing can be a lonely endeavor without community. I'd like to express my appreciation to my long-time writing buddies Elizabeth MacBride, Anne Field, and Eilene Zimmerman for their input, advice and support and for being there all of these years. Thanks, too, to my friends June Avignone and Gregory Van Maanen for inspiring me with their passion for creating. Thank you, as well, to entrepreneur John Khalil for the thoughtful feedback.

My late sister-in-law, Eileen Sicoli, passed away before this book took shape, but her bravery and commitment to what really mattered made a lasting impression on me that greatly influenced this book.

Finally, I truly appreciate the support, encouragement, practical help, and insights from my family during the many hours I devoted to this project. Thank you to my brother, Michael, for the ideas and input. And, finally, a big hug to my husband, Bob, and my children Anna, Emily, Sarah, and Robert. I could not have written this book without you there to remind me, every day, of what is most important to me: my family.

INTRODUCTION

Click on almost any headline about the gig economy, and you'll come across a fierce debate. Supporters of the traditional job see the world of free agents as one where capitalism has run amok, leaving hapless workers to fight each other for scraps of work—as they cling to the slippery rock of middle-class life. Champions of what author Dan Pink called the Free Agent Nation see a very different reality, in which former wage slaves can ditch their cramped cubicles in hermetically sealed offices for a life in which they control their schedule, destiny, and income.

The truth is, we don't know yet what a world of increasingly independent work will mean. We've never had as many free agents as we do today. As of 2010, the United States Government Accountability Office says that 40% of US workers have "alternative" work arrangements in their main jobs, meaning they are freelancers, temps, contractors, contract company workers or part-timers.[1] That is unprecedented—and it's a change that's happening in industrialized nations around the world.

Many people worry that these workers will struggle without giant employers helping them to run their work lives and keep their paychecks steady. That's a valid concern. But another equally important point is what this growing army of free agents can accomplish on their own. Armed with the right knowledge and mindset, could they create something even better for themselves than the traditional "secure" job? Will they be better off without powerful gatekeepers deciding the fate of their careers? Will they have a greater chance of reaching their true potential and attaining a higher income in a world where they drive their own careers and a boss can't subtly penalize them for being too young, too old, a mom, a member of a minority group, a person with a disability, a caregiver, a committed Little League coach, someone who wants to work from home, or any of the other reasons people get slow-tracked at work, regardless of their talents and contributions?

I am a former senior editor at *Fortune Small Business* magazine and have contributed to *Fortune, Money, CNBC, Forbes, Inc.*, and many other publications. Based on my experience interviewing hundreds of entrepreneurs every year, I believe the vast majority of self-employed people have barely begun to unlock their potential in making the most of their businesses. That potential may be even greater than we imagine. Not long ago I spoke with Eric Scott, a partner at SciFi VC, a venture capital firm in San Francisco, founded by Max Levchin, cofounder of PayPal.

---

1 *Contingent Workforce: Size, Characteristics, Earnings, and Benefits*. Published: April 20, 2015. Pages 15–16. Public release: May 20, 2015. Available online at gao.gov/products/GAO-15-168R

Scott told me he and his colleagues have been asking themselves how much longer it will be until a one-person firm gets acquired for $1 billion.

As we figure out where it is possible to take a one-person business, the question is how to help free agents make a great living. Most of today's free agents have been thrust into running a one-person business without any preparation. Universities have a vested interest in selling the idea that all of their graduates will be working as high-paying, full-time employees at well-known companies. Outside of entrepreneurship programs, they rarely broach the possibility that their students may end up working for themselves nor do they teach skills that will help them thrive in self-employment. It's easy to see why schools don't want to talk about this. How many parents would willingly pay the huge annual tuition bills if they knew their children might essentially be signing up for Freelancing 101 and a life of scrambling for projects? And how many students would be willing to take out tens of thousands of dollars in student loans if the promise after graduation was not, in fact, a cool job at Google but a part-time position at a little-known company where the pay is so low they will have to drive for Uber on the side? In reality, many graduates are patching together their income this way, as the world of employment rapidly changes, but have yet to master how to thrive in self-employment.

Meanwhile, midcareer workers find themselves increasingly insecure, as their companies look to cut costs by outsourcing overseas, automating work once done by people, and replacing full-timers with contractors. Recently, I attended a presentation by a coworking space provider that usually caters to freelancers and startups. One growth area, its executives said, is the renting out of entire floors and even whole buildings to companies employing traditional workers. These clients want to be free to expand and contract their workforce more often than a standard lease allows. Even if the employees who sit in the coworking space view their jobs as permanent, clearly the employers don't see things the same way. At the same time, many companies are increasingly candid about the fact that their plans for traditional staffing are built around "junior" talent. That's good news when you're looking for your first job, but it means that with each birthday, promotion, and salary bump, employees in these firms are a little closer to getting squeezed out of their jobs. Many workers might do better running a solo business than climbing the shaky career ladder, if they have the know-how to do so very successfully.

Theoretically, there are plenty of places outside of school to learn how to run a business. But if you turn to the experts in your local startup ecosystem, you'll very likely hear that to succeed, you've got to "scale" a business into a job-creating machine—and if you don't want to, you're not ambitious enough. "The thinking is that it's better to invest in ten people who are going to grow their businesses to a very large size than in one hundred people who are going to run single-person businesses," says Donna Kelley, a professor of entrepreneurship at Babson College. Many programs run by government and financial services firms that serve small business also view one-person firms as duds—run by people who failed to become job creators because they think too small. Their emphasis is on reprogramming solo entrepreneurs out of mindsets—like not delegating enough—that keep them from hiring people.

But consider this: Out of more than twenty-eight million small businesses in the United States, twenty-three million are "non-employers," meaning no one has a job there except the owners.[2] I believe most have actively opted out of hiring employees for a simple reason: they don't want to. And there is nothing wrong with that.

There is something wonderful and exciting in the fact that millions of independent spirits in the United States have taken the initiative to create jobs for themselves, doing exactly what they want to do. Not everyone wants to be Elon Musk, dreaming up the next Tesla, nor is everyone cut out to be a boss. Many people start businesses to gain control over their time and enjoy independence—a freedom that can slip away as an organization grows. And this is a conscious choice. "They are doing it because they prefer to, not because they have to," says Kelley, who has studied businesses around the world as leader of the US research team for the sweeping *Global Entrepreneurship Monitor* study.[3] "As society becomes more advanced, people are more likely to do the jobs and work they want."

Nonetheless, the lives of many free agents are more difficult than they need to be, often because they don't know how to make a great living. They need to make good money because they have no safety net. The system just isn't set up for them. Industrial economies are built around the idea that workers will be employees with traditional jobs. Though solo business owners pay taxes like

2 *United States Small Business Profile, 2016.* SBA Office of Advocacy. Available online at sba.gov/sites/default/files/advocacy/United_States.pdf

3 Global Entrepreneurship Monitor studies are available online at gemconsortium.org/report

everyone else, they typically don't get access to programs like unemployment if their work dries up. In the United States, health care is generally very expensive to buy on your own—and efforts to reform the system have been very contentious. Transactions like buying a house can also be very difficult if you earn your income from freelance jobs, rather than a traditional one, because of banks' requirements that you prove your income. These hassles and extra costs can start to wear on freelancers. I can attest to this, having lived for about a decade as part of a two-freelancer couple with four kids. Before my husband very recently accepted an in-house position with a client, we bought our family's health insurance through a broker or directly through an insurance company—and the premiums were akin to mortgage payments.

Does it have to be this way? I've often wondered why no one in national politics pays serious attention to the millions of workers who earn their living outside of traditional jobs.

Through my reporting, I have met some independent entrepreneurs whose stories persuaded me that maybe we don't have to wait for the system to recognize and value the independently employed. By building their one-person businesses and partnerships to $1 million in annual revenue or more (or, in a few cases, very close), these workers generate enough income after taxes and expenses to insulate themselves from the hassles that many free agents face and to multiply the freedoms and rewards exponentially. What are they doing to make a living? All kinds of things that tap into their personal passions—selling organic honey, teaching online classes, marketing ebooks, investing in real estate, and even running traditional businesses in fields like consulting.

In the pages ahead, you'll learn how these owners have grown their revenue in ultra-lean businesses, so you can apply their ideas to starting or growing a business of your own. Some have become devoted to the idea of remaining a one-person business for the long term. Others have found that creating an ultra-lean, high-revenue startup opened up exciting opportunities they had not expected—including scaling up in the traditional way when they were ready for it. That's why you'll see, in some of their stories, that they did eventually become employers—when it made good sense for them and for the business to do so. In some cases, they had to consider labor laws when making decisions about how to grow. (If you need hourly shift workers, for instance, they generally can't be hired as contractors.)

If you aspire to creating your own million-dollar, one-person business, view this book as the crash course you never got in school. Even if you never hit $1 million—or don't aspire to—understanding the smart and creative ways these owners run their businesses will help you achieve your personal goals and realize your potential a lot more quickly, so you have more time and energy to do the things you love. You'll have the knowledge to consider a brand-new career option you might have never realized was available to you. There's no reason to wing it on your own when you have guides like these amazing entrepreneurs to show you the way.

1

THE MILLION-DOLLAR, ONE-PERSON REVOLUTION

Laszlo Nadler, thirty-six when I spoke with him, lives a life many dream of: he is on track to bring in more than $2 million a year in a profitable business that is a one-man show. Nadler runs a five-year-old online store, Tools4Wisdom, from his home in New Jersey. The store sells inspirational weekly and monthly planners. Nadler outsources the printing, so most of his daily work consists of customer service, business development, and marketing. The business leaves plenty of time to get away for vacations with his wife and two young daughters.

Nadler never planned to be an entrepreneur. He studied business management and technology and then built a career as a project manager for one of the top trading units at a multinational bank. It was a good job that seemed to justify the college tuition his parents had paid and enabled him to support his young family. And yet, as Nadler was talking with his oldest daughter about the importance of doing what you love almost six years ago, his words sounded hollow. He realized he was not following his own advice.

He liked his work well enough, but he was under constant pressure to meet deadlines and often in intense situations. Parachuting from one trading crisis to the next at the bank was not what he truly loved. What did excite him—and had led to his career in project management—was improving his own productivity and helping the people around him do the same. Nadler decided it was time to actually follow the advice he had given his daughter and soon started a side business, designing and producing his own planners and selling them online. Unlike most daybooks, his planners are not built around making to-do lists. Instead, they focus you on the essential outcomes each week that will move you toward your primary goals. His approach to time management is different, too, focusing on how much mental energy people have each day rather than on how many hours there are to squeeze activities into. "I realized after all of these years that it's not time units we have, but attention units," he says. "You may have three to four hours of true attention units per day."

Many people loved his idea and bought the planners. When his income from the planners hit six figures a little under two years ago, he quit his job to work on the business full-time.

Nadler is part of an exciting trend: the growth of ultra-lean, one-person businesses that are reaching and exceeding $1 million in revenue. According to recent statistics released by the US Census Bureau, in 2015 there were 35,584 "nonemployer" firms— that is, those that do not employ anyone other than the owners— that brought in $1 million to $2,499,999 in annual revenue. That's up 5.8% from 2014, 18% from 2013, 21% from 2012 and 33%

from 2011. Some elite nonemployer businesses are even exceeding these revenues. In 2015, 2,090 businesses had annual receipts of $2.5 million to $4.99 million, and 355 businesses brought in $5 million or more.

While these numbers are still relatively small, many more of these tiny businesses are approaching the $1 million mark. Many have strong potential to break $1 million:

- 258,148 firms brought in $500,000 to $999,999.
- 584,586 generated $250,000 to $499,999 in revenue.
- 1,861,656 businesses brought in $100,000 to $249,999.

What's driving their growth? One factor is the internet, which has enabled individual entrepreneurs to plunge into a vast global marketplace cheaply and quickly. "It has provided a whole set of capabilities and tools these entrepreneurs can access," says Andrew Karpie, who studies online platforms used in the labor sector as research director, services and labor procurement/supply chain, at Spend Matters Network, a research, analysis, and media firm focused on procurement of technology and innovation.

The capabilities available to entrepreneurs in one-person operations are vast. It has become much easier to quickly set up a business's legal structure, operations, and distribution, says venture capitalist Eric Scott. If entrepreneurs want to form a business entity, they can do so in under an hour through a host of online legal services providers. To put up a website, they can turn to free and inexpensive platforms like WordPress, Squarespace, and Weebly; find any design help they need on online platforms, such as 99designs; and locate any necessary writing or tech talent on a freelance marketplace, such as Upwork, Freelancer, or

PeoplePerHour. Thanks to cloud-based storage, buying expensive servers—once a huge barrier to entry for startups—is no longer mandatory. On top of this, relatively low-cost digital advertising on social platforms like Facebook and search engines like Google makes it easy to reach a huge audience quickly. And once entrepreneurs find customers, it is easy to process payments from any corner of the world online, through a fast-growing army of service providers, in some cases simply by clicking on an option that lets them accept ACH or credit card payments through their invoicing software.

But solo business owners' capacity to scale their efforts isn't just about the growth of free and automated tools. It also reflects a shift in attitudes. Rather than adopt Henry Ford–era business models, in which scaling up depends on hiring legions of employees, these entrepreneurs choose to travel light. When they need to expand their individual capabilities, they often deliberately turn to contractors or firms that handle billing and other outsourceable functions. As Alex Hood, vice president of Intuit's QuickBooks Online, explained at the Smart Hustle Small Business Conference, because of such trends, the average size of small businesses in America has shrunk from 6.5 employees in 2001 to 4 in 2014.

As ultra-lean firms grow, so do the businesses of the contractors and outsourced providers they hire. Some entrepreneurs find that relying on these outside providers creates a more positive, egalitarian relationship than many managers have with their staff. These entrepreneurs see the people who support them as trusted partners, not direct reports whom they have to supervise. They are all part of a community of individuals who are building businesses simultaneously and symbiotically.

"I realized how much more contractors and entrepreneurs are willing to do a better job for you," says Dan Mezheritsky, thirty-three, founder and president of Fitness on the Go, a one-person in-home personal training franchise headquartered in Vancouver, Canada. "They are trying to help your business—and grow theirs—as opposed to an employee who is just there for a paycheck." Fitness on the Go generated about $5.5 million in revenue in 2016, with $1.5 million of that for corporate headquarters alone and about 30% of the $1.5 million as profit.

While the Census Bureau's name—nonemployer firms—defines these ultra-lean businesses by what they are not, many entrepreneurs clearly see them for what they are: an engine that offers the potential for high income and a balanced, interesting life—on their own terms. These businesses offer three things that elude most workers today: control over their time, enough money to enjoy it, and the independence to live life as they want.

Many entrepreneurs take one of two employee-development paths to economic freedom: (1) quitting their job and launching a traditional small business, such as a shop or a restaurant, or (2) trying to scale a startup into the next company to go public or get acquired by a big corporation. But the million-dollar, one-person business entrepreneurs have embraced a new, third path—one in which a single individual or business partners can extend their capabilities to achieve what it would normally take a larger team to do. What they're pulling off takes effort, but the changing nature of work, the growth of automation, and technological developments that unlock market access are making it easier by the day. "There is a way of thinking that scales beyond them," says

Eric Scott. The way they run a business makes its impact and reach far greater than the sum of its parts.

So who are the entrepreneurs behind these businesses? And what exactly are they doing to make money? **The founders of million-dollar, one-person businesses and partnerships are every-day people who have grown very smart about making the most of the time they spend working.** Solo businesses that hit the million-dollar range typically fall into six categories:

1 E-commerce
2 Manufacturing
3 Informational content creation
4 Professional services and creative businesses, such as marketing firms, public speaking businesses, and consultancies
5 Personal services firms, offering expertise, such as fitness coaching
6 Real estate

These companies use outsourcing, automation, mobile technology, or a combination of all three to build, operate, and grow their businesses. In covering them for various publications, I've found that no two are alike; a brief roundup of companies that you'll read more about later underscores this:

Rebecca Krones, thirty-eight, and her husband, Luis Zevallos, fifty-four, run Tropical Traders Specialty Foods, a business in Oakland, California, that has generated more than $1 million a year selling organic honey through their website and various retail channels. Outsourcing the packing of the honey gives them plenty of time to spend with their two young children.

Cory Binsfield, fifty-two, brings in more than $1 million a year from the rent on 116 apartments he owns in Duluth, Minnesota. He bought his first property when he was a young financial planner, making barely $50,000 a year. At the time, he couldn't get a bank loan, so he persuaded the owner to let him put down $5,000 and lend him the rest of the money to buy it. He slowly built the track record that enabled him to get a bank loan two years later and buy his next property—and many more after that. "I had it mapped out," he explains. "Buy ten duplexes—ten two-families—and I could easily be a millionaire. I hit that target within five years." And he just kept at it.

Meghan Telpner, thirty-seven, runs MeghanTelpner.com, a wellness site, which she started nine years ago after recovering from an autoimmune disease that left her too ill to work in her advertising career. After completing her certification in holistic nutrition, she began teaching cooking classes in the Toronto loft where she lived. Three years ago, she took her classes online, launching the Academy of Culinary Nutrition (CulinaryNutrition.com), where she shares culinary training with nutritionists and others who are trying to eat healthy. Her business hit the $1 million mark one year after she launched her online school.

Jonathan Johnson, fifty-seven, worked in real estate finance until he foresaw the global financial collapse and started his business, DirectGov Source Inc., in Chico, California, as a new way of generating income. He generated $2.8 million in 2016 and turned a profit selling equipment like ballistic vests and riot helmets to law enforcement agencies and by creating another site that sells infection-exposure control kits to medical and home health-care facilities.

Kelly Lester, a mother of three who is in her fifties, owns EasyLunchboxes, which sells her bento box–style lunch-packing containers through a major internet marketplace and her own website, generating more than $1 million a year through this profitable venture. That gives her time for her other passion: acting in motion pictures, TV, and live theater. She recently made a deal to sell her lunchboxes in more than nine hundred Target stores across the country.

Sol Orwell, thirty-two, who lives in downtown Toronto, takes in a seven-figure revenue selling ebooks on nutritional supplements, which he hires expert contractors, such as nutrition researchers, to write. He sells them via a site called Examine.com. Orwell spends his abundant free time traveling the world. On an ordinary day when he is working at home, he satisfies his desire to be on the move by going for extended walks without feeling compelled to get back to his desk and actively earn more.

Many people running one- or two-person businesses never realize it is possible to generate $1 million or more in revenue from them—or they don't know how to pull it off. *The Million-Dollar, One-Person Business* will show you how to do so, drawing on the stories of real people who have hit the mark. You will learn a system to do three things:

1 Identify the high-revenue, one-person business best suited to your interests, skills, and experience from the five main types.
2 Launch the business successfully, no matter how little startup money you have, using low-cost and easily accessible distribution channels.

3 Keep the business humming so you can enjoy your life
   outside of work and give back.

Will a million-dollar, one-person business bring you a lifestyle
in which you never have to look at a price tag again? Probably not.
And it won't get you $1 million in annual *income*, because you will
have to subtract your overhead and taxes (ouch!). But it should
enable you to pocket a generous six-figure income. And even if
you don't need to make $1 million in revenue, these ideas will
help you earn more in less time, so you can enjoy the rest of your
life more. If you live in an area with a high cost of living, that'll
buy you what many people can no longer afford on the stagnating
income from traditional jobs:

- Home ownership (without fear that you can't pay
  the mortgage)
- Retirement savings
- Student loan debt repayment
- The ability to pay for college
- The freedom and means to take time off and travel
  when it suits you

Even better, you will be able to bring home that money
without making the personal sacrifices that come with earning
the equivalent income in a corporate job. **In a million-dollar, one-person business, you can be part of the world outside of your office every day of the week, without fearing that taking the time to do fun things after work or meet your family responsibilities will hurt your career or get you axed if the company downsizes.** You will have
plenty of time for the interesting people in your life. You will
not miss the first ten years of your child's life, as many corporate

executives and even entrepreneurs running midsize companies regretfully acknowledge they have. Having more space in your life for adventure and relationships is a real possibility — and, for many people, one that is both exciting and a little daunting.

2

WHAT MAKES MILLION-DOLLAR, ONE-PERSON BUSINESSES WORK

Laszlo Nadler, the entrepreneur who started the planner business Tools4Wisdom, took an economic leap bigger than many people can imagine taking. He went from working in a steady, though not especially high-paying, job in project management to selling daily planners he developed. Instead of getting home at eight on weeknights after solving the latest crisis at work, he now has time to think about big-picture questions like: "What are my five-year goals—and what creative steps will it take to accomplish them?" He also has plenty of time every day of the week to spend with his wife and their two daughters.

When Nadler started, he had no idea how to run a business. And he had no desire to be an e-commerce entrepreneur—one of those six potential routes to creating a million-dollar business. His goal was to create a side income by creating a truly automated business that would give him the freedom to choose to work—or not—on any given day. An online store, he realized, was the quickest and easiest route to doing that. "*The 4-Hour Workweek* got me started," he says, referring to Tim Ferriss's best-selling book. "I was inspired to hack the system, to question the status quo and see if I [could] pull it off myself—and behold, it works."

Tools4Wisdom, Nadler's startup, is one of my favorite examples of the million-dollar, one-person business, but there are many similar ones springing up every day. Let's look at Nadler's business type, e-commerce. As of 2015, there were 2,965 retail businesses with no employees other than the owners that brought in $1 million to $2.49 million in revenue annually, 571 powerhouses that brought in $2.5 million to $4.99 million, and six superstars that brought in $5 million or more. Those are still small numbers, but there were many more retailers churning out six-figure revenues with no employees. Consider this: 20,567 were bringing in $500,000 to $999,999; 52,213 were pulling in $250,000 to $499,999, and 131,919 were generating $100,000 to $249,999. Many of these retailers are internet stores. There were 35,501 retailers breaking six- or seven-figure revenues in the government category that includes internet stores, "electronic shopping," and "mail-order houses." And these tiny shops often do more than create an income for the owners: they can become valuable assets that can be sold, as we'll get into later.

SUCCESS FACTORS

Certainly, there are many internet stores that either never get past $5,000 in revenue or plateau at a level of sales, such as $25,000, that most people can't live on. That is also true of many independent businesses, from graphic design shops to consultancies. Nadler's business is a good example of what distinguishes the successful ones. Understanding what separates them will help you make the most of what you'll learn in the chapters to come about identifying the right business idea; turning that concept into a high-revenue, one-person business; and living the lifestyle you choose at the same time.

THE REAL UPSIDE

Freedom and independence usually top the list when self-employed people and entrepreneurs are asked what they like best about going out on their own. Among independent workers surveyed for *The State of Independence in America 2017* report by MBO Partners,[4] a company in Herndon, Virginia, that provides back-office services to independent workers, 75% said the freedom to be their own boss motivated them to do independent work, and 74% named having more flexibility.

4 MBO Partners, Inc., *The State of Independence in America 2017* report. Available online at mbopartners.com/state-of-independence

Many solo entrepreneurs also make more money than they did in their traditional jobs. MBO Partners counted 16.2 million full-time independent workers in the United States in the survey of 3,008 residents ages 21 and older, which was conducted by Emergent Research and Rockbridge Associates. These full-time independents averaged over 35 hours a week of work and put in at least 15 hours weekly. Among those surveyed, 43% said they make more money working for themselves. A substantial 19.75% of them—3.2 million people—earned more than $100,000 in 2017, up 4.9% from 2016 alone. They can pull it off because they have paid careful attention to the expertise and services that are valued in the marketplace in coming up with their own business models. "You are seeing the number of people that have higher level skills that are in demand really growing rapidly," says Gene Zaino, president and CEO of MBO Partners. As the research also showed, most people doing independent work chose to do so and weren't forced into it by a layoff or other crisis. Reflecting this, MBO Partners has predicted that by 2022 the number of independent workers in America will hit 47.6 million, up from 40.9 million today. If the US working population ages 16 and older remains at its current 123,761,000 people, that figure will represent 38% of all workers.[5]

---

5 Bureau of Labor Statistics. "Labor Force Statistics from the Current Population Survey." Available online at bls.gov/cps/cpsaat08.htm

Owners of million-dollar, one-person businesses do have a few key aspects in common; let's take a closer look.

GEEKDOM

Million-dollar entrepreneurs understand that no matter how lucrative their idea or what their market research proves, they won't stick with it if they aren't truly interested in it. When Nadler looked for the right business idea, he searched for clues in his daily life and concluded that his near-obsessive fascination with daily planning tools would be a good place to start. The more Nadler improved his own productivity in his project management career, the more content he established for his business idea. Realizing he'd never found a paper planner that focused on people's big-picture goals in the way he wanted, Nadler decided to design and sell his own version.

Is selling planners right for every entrepreneur? No. For some people, even thinking about a daily planner would be a form of slow torture. If what you obsess about is electronic gadgets, stock market investing, Paleo cooking, funky handbags, or ceramic garden gnomes, your million-dollar business idea probably has something to do with that interest. **Uncovering an idea that you will enjoy thinking about every day—whether that is when you are writing copy for your website or answering a customer's question about it—is the secret.** Of course, you need to do your market research to make sure there are other people interested in buying what you plan to sell. You can't build a million-dollar, one-person business around a passion that only ten people on the planet share, unless you have achieved such elite status in your niche that people will be willing to pay you very high prices.

DITCH THE DIY

Most solo business owners do almost everything themselves. There's nothing inherently wrong with being hands-on if you love the work you're doing, but that approach won't get you to $1 million in revenue. **What will help you break into the seven figures is to expand your capacity beyond what one person can do.** The only ways to do that, without hiring employees, are by hiring contractors to help you, outsourcing, and automating some of your work. Most high-revenue, nonemployer business owners use some combination of all three strategies. As Nadler puts it, "You need a team to accomplish your dream. If your dream does not have a team, it is not big enough." You also need to price your product or services correctly, as we'll get to later.

Nadler is a master of creating an ultra-lean team. Early on, he had a vision for how he wanted his planners to look, but he had no training in design. He could have tried to teach himself design, which may have been fun. However, mastering it would have taken years and could have sapped his energy, preventing him from ever starting his business. Staying focused on his vision to create a high-revenue business that would help him leave corporate America, he resisted the temptation to do it himself, and, after some experimenting on his own with his products' designs, he hired a local freelance graphic designer to help him create original designs with a unique vibe. He didn't have to look far to find a designer. When hiring someone to clean his house, he had unknowingly chosen a recent MBA graduate with a passion for design. When he learned of her other talents, he enlisted her help in perfecting his planners. Designing the original planner pages in Excel, he had the designer translate them into Adobe InDesign. He has since found other freelancers by making a practice of looking for hidden talents in the people he meets in his daily life, in case they, too, might appreciate a chance to help him in his business.

Soon after he had designs he liked, Nadler began printing them in his home office in his free time, testing them himself to see how well they worked and experimenting with the production. Unaware of what manufacturing the planners at home would actually entail, after seven to ten months, he realized that the DIY approach didn't work for production either. "I created a printer farm to test my products," he says. "I had twelve or fourteen high-end laser printers. Then came the holidays. While everyone was celebrating, I was creating my own one-person sweatshop. I finally found a reliable supplier. That's when business took off." The supplier was an online printing company.

Nadler's efforts paid off, and now he is focused on growing his business. **"If you can outsource your supply chain, you have almost unlimited scaling available,"** he explains.

SIMPLIFY SELLING AND FULFILLMENT

Nadler created his website himself using Shopify, an e-commerce platform, to design and develop a simple online store, but he never focused his attention there. **Most million-dollar entrepreneurs experiment for a while with finding the best way to sell, but they ultimately select one method or outlet that works best.** Nadler decided to submit an application to market his planners on a major internet marketplace that would give him good exposure to customers. By selling on the giant retail site, he could use that vendor's fulfillment service, so he wouldn't have to pack and ship orders himself. Fortunately, he already had a product to test, which the marketplace requires when sellers apply, so he didn't have to invest much more in the business to get started. All he needed was a professional selling account for $49 a month. Fortunately, Nadler was quickly approved as a seller.

NURTURE A COMMUNITY

Though million-dollar entrepreneurs don't have a boss or employees, they don't thrive in isolation. They understand their success depends on people, from vendors and freelance talent to clients. **Typically, the success of these businesses is based heavily on connecting with customers who are passionate about what they sell and have the power to get other people excited about purchasing it, too.**

Nadler turned to free digital tools to help him build a community around his planners. For instance, Facebook Audience Insights helped him get a detailed demographic profile of the buyers he needed to target; he discovered they were mostly middle-aged women. Armed with this information, he kept tinkering with his product descriptions and other marketing details until they were effective and sales took off.

To keep the business thriving, now that it is his sole source of income, Nadler spends 80% of his time focusing on growth, which for his product means making sure every customer is happy enough to spread the word about Tools4Wisdom. It is a different approach from the one that many conventional businesses take: handing off customer service to entry-level employees or a team of ill-trained call-center workers. "Customer service has become the number one driver of my day-to-day activities," Nadler says—because the reviews in the online marketplace drive new sales. "When you have 110 reviews and someone wants to buy a product, guess which one they read first? The one star."

SEEING WORK DIFFERENTLY

Nadler's and others' one-person business success isn't just about focusing on growth. It's even more important to adopt a fresh way of thinking about work, one that reflects the new technology-enabled possibilities.

Like most people fortunate enough to live in developed economies, Nadler is influenced by societal pressure to take the "safe" route to support himself and his family: a traditional company job. In the United States that usually means dutifully stiff-upper-lipping it through a stressful commute to an office where the daily routine, while occasionally stimulating, is often full of boring and pointless meetings and other wastes of one's limited time on earth. Too often, it also entails reporting to a difficult boss who controls workload and opportunity.

Nadler views running his own business as a more exciting and optimistic path, even though there is some risk involved. "There are two types of people," he says. "One prefers security over success and is comfortable in an environment where they can predict the outcome. They are perfect for the employee career track. The other is the entrepreneur. They are open to exploring and are not worried as much about the outcome. They are looking forward to the journey." As Nadler began running his part-time side business, he realized he was a person who enjoyed the journey more than the security. He shook off his past notions of how he should live and embraced being a solo entrepreneur, reading widely from websites and books that reminded him of what truly matters most in his life and helped him stay committed to his path when there was no societal GPS to guide him.

Nadler's calculated bet paid off. Just four years into running his still-profitable business full-time, he broke $2 million in revenue—and has seen his life transformed. Will Nadler still be running an ultra-lean operation a year or two from now—or leading a fast-growing team? That isn't what's most important about his story. **The point of the million-dollar, one-person business is that it gives you choices—whether to keep it small while earning a great income or to continue growing it.** Neither path, you'll notice, involves the pain of struggling in a marginal freelance business, a situation in which common unexpected expenses, such as having to buy a new set of tires, can put you behind for months.

Nadler's advice to other would-be entrepreneurs who want to enjoy the freedom he does? Recognize that what you learned in school about work hasn't caught up with the new, exciting and high-paying opportunities for making a living that the digital era has brought. Choose early to educate yourself on subjects *you* love and then become an expert at them by practicing your passion daily.

Are you ready to trade the stale ways of working for one that will enable you to experience the freedom that entrepreneurs like Nadler enjoy every day? Sol Orwell and the other entrepreneurs you'll meet in the next chapter will show you how to figure out which business will enable you to do that.

3

WHAT BUSINESS
COULD YOU START?

Sol Orwell, thirty-two, the Toronto ebooks entrepreneur you met in the first chapter, is a global citizen. Originally from Pakistan, he grew up mostly in Saudi Arabia and Japan, and then in Houston, Texas, and Canada, where his father's work as an engineer for an oil company took the family. Passionate about seeing more of the world, Orwell now spends three or four months of the year traveling.

Orwell has carefully constructed his business, Examine.com, to support and accommodate his travel lifestyle. He has deliberately kept the business lean and free of outside investment, so he is the only one setting milestones and deadlines for the company. To keep his schedule open, he hires a trusted contractor to manage the business for him, giving his collaborator a small equity stake to keep him motivated.

"To me, traveling is much more important than making a lot of money," Orwell explained. "Next week, I'm going away for four days to a music festival. The next week, I'll be away for four days for a bachelor party. The next two weeks, I'll be in Sweden. That would not be possible if I brought in VCs [venture capitalists]. I don't feel I need a $5 million house, fancy cars, or fancy watches. I don't begrudge anyone who wants that lifestyle. Traveling is the main thing I focus on." Thanks to a profitable business that has broken the seven-figure revenue mark, he has enough money to explore that passion. And because of all the friends he has met through the internet and on social media, he has connections around the world to visit in his travels.

He also gives back. When we last spoke, he was raising money for the nonprofit group Community Food Centres Canada at an event for entrepreneurs called the Sausage Showdown. Attendees were asked to pay $100 to attend the event, which covered all of the sausage they could eat, prepared by high-end chefs. Orwell put up the $2,000 to cover the overhead, so all proceeds would go to the nonprofit. "If my two-thousand-dollar investment brings in ten thousand dollars as a charitable donation, suddenly I've five-timesed my charitable investment," says Orwell. The Sausage Showdown was a follow-up to an earlier, very popular fund-raising event he organized called the Chocolate Chip Cookie Off, in which professional chefs competed to bake the best chocolate chip cookie.

So how do you get from where you currently are in your career to enjoying the freedom Orwell has? **It starts with forming an idea of the type of business you want to run and the lifestyle you want it to support.**

That isn't something you can do in one afternoon. For most of the entrepreneurs profiled in this book, it took some deep thinking, soul searching, market research, and experimenting. Orwell, for instance, tried four other types of businesses—online gaming, domain names, local search, and daily deals—with varying degrees of success before he found one that would get him to $1 million with no employees. That required commitment, but it also brought him big rewards. You'll find worksheets in the Appendices (pages 171–205) that will help you through the thinking process and narrow down the list of potential businesses to the one that will help you build your own high-revenue, one-person enterprise.

FINDING YOUR SEVEN-FIGURE SOLO BUSINESS: Q&A WITH MEGHAN TELPNER

It's not easy to identify the type of one-person business you can grow to $1 million in revenue and more. It's a different process from finding a business that will allow you to earn a little extra money or replace a job. The point is to find a business that enables you to multiply the financial impact of your own efforts without taking on the high overhead that comes with running a business the traditional way.

Million-dollar entrepreneurs tend to follow their own unique and often serendipitous path to finding the right idea, whether by tapping into knowledge they've picked up in a previous career, responding to a gap in the marketplace they've observed as a consumer, or building on knowledge they've built in a fledgling business.

Here are some suggestions from Meghan Telpner—the self-described "nutritionista" we met in chapter 1. In addition to running her wellness website and the Academy of Culinary Nutrition, Telpner coaches other business owners and has unique insights into the challenges they face in coming up with the right concept.

How can budding entrepreneurs identify interests they can turn into a business they would enjoy?

Telpner: Running a passion-based business is the most difficult thing in the world and potentially the most lucrative and rewarding. Not all of our hobbies and everything we love to do need to be part of our business. It's important that you believe in what you want to create and what you'll be selling and also that you take your time to build a solid foundation on which it can grow, while also allowing you to become better at what you do and understanding what is and isn't working in your business. We're inundated in social media with promotions for six-figure launches and list-building strategies, but if we're not building on our credibility, integrity, and experience, it may be a one-time thing. A slow and steady approach can help ensure that this year's six-figure launch can be a seven-figure business in two or three years.

Do you have any favorite tools for researching business ideas?

Telpner: The thing that makes us a special snowflake needs to be part of our business in some way. Most of us don't know what that thing is because it comes so easily to us, or it just seems too obvious. If we can combine that with a strong "Why?" in terms of why we actually want to do this in the first place (and this can't be just a money motivator), that is going to help. Lastly, we need to be either solving a problem, filling a need, or doing it better, in a measurable way, than what's already out there.

Did you do market research? If so, how did you go about it?

Telpner: I do very informal market research, usually through long-format blog posts. I'll do in-depth research into a topic, write a 2,500-word blog post, share it across social media channels, and see what the response is like. Based on that, I may take that information and expand it further into a webinar or live keynote or develop an online program. Mostly I take to heart comments that are posted and questions that are asked through social media and email and use that as inspiration for where to focus my program development.

Do you have any suggestions for people in content-oriented businesses on packaging their knowledge for sale?

Telpner: We each have a specific set of skills and approaches that make how we do what we do unique. This is what we need to leverage. I don't think we need to overthink this. If we have a content-based business, we should have a pretty good idea of what our audience loves and responds to. The best way to tap into this is to participate in the community we have built, rather than be just the content generator. Engage in conversation with your community, and ask them what they want. If what they say lines up with something you actually want to create, then you know you'll be launching something with a built-in customer base. Making that thing really awesome—from how you describe and market it (under-promise, over-deliver, and be honest in your portrayal) to how you execute it (no detail is too small!) and the follow-up you do later (because you genuinely care how your customers/clients receive and engage with what you are selling) will determine how much your audience will share and talk about it and help bring in new leads and sales. This can also determine how successful your next product will be.

THE PATH TO FINDING YOUR MILLION-DOLLAR IDEA

As Telpner points out, there is no premapped route to finding your million-dollar idea, but many entrepreneurs use a common process to create high-revenue, one-person businesses.

RIGHT-SIZE YOUR GOALS

The mainstream business press celebrates entrepreneurs—such as Mark Zuckerberg of Facebook, Elon Musk of Tesla, and Sergey Brin and Larry Page of Google—who scale their ideas into substantial-size businesses. Great entrepreneurs' stories are inspiring, but they can also be intimidating. **It's easy to think that if you don't have an idea as big as Facebook and your goal is not world domination or a billion-dollar market capitalization, it's not worth going into business at all.**

Because of this conditioning, many people talk themselves out of pursuing a business that might allow them to live a much more rewarding and fulfilling life. That's a little like telling yourself that because you don't swim at the level of Michael Phelps, you should give up on a lifelong dream of competing in a triathlon—and that you might as well give up on swimming laps at the gym and sit on the couch watching swimming on TV instead. Aiming high is great, and it's important to think big if your goal is to break $1 million in revenue, but not to the point that it immobilizes you and prevents you from going after an interesting work life built around your passions.

Martin Goh, thirty-nine, and his wife Carlene, thirty-seven, realized the importance of setting the goals that mattered most to them after she was diagnosed in 2013 at age thirty-three with stage IV, non–small-cell lung cancer. They had been married only since 2008. After Carlene underwent treatment and her health stabilized, the couple, based in Singapore, began to reflect on life and realized they really wanted to become entrepreneurs. "What we wanted to do was to have a go at starting our own business, so that we could do something together and have a more flexible lifestyle that allows us a little more time with each other," says Martin.

Both had been working in corporate jobs, and Martin wondered if they could succeed as entrepreneurs. "One of the biggest things that convinced me for the longest time that I shouldn't start my own business was I thought I had to have a killer idea," says Martin. "I had to have something no one else had thought of, and if not, there was no point. Then I realized about a year ago how silly that thinking was. How many monopolistic markets are there in the world? Every market supports more than one player."

The Gohs took a leap of faith and started The Local Fella in May 2016, leaving their jobs behind. They are Christians, and the decision followed "quite a bit of prayer," says Martin. At the time of my most recent conversation with the Gohs, Carlene's tumors had stabilized, but she still had cancer, and they had to be mindful of this.

They live in Singapore, and the business they ultimately started provides customized travel guides for visitors to Singapore, selling them for the price of a guidebook. Travelers complete a survey on their goals for their trip, and the Gohs help them plan it by tapping their local knowledge, saving their customers time on research and ensuring an insider travel experience.

Fortunately, by living with Martin's parents to avoid high housing costs for several years, the Gohs saved money that has given them the financial freedom they needed to get their idea off the ground. Of course, moving in with Mom and Dad isn't practical for every entrepreneur. It's still very possible to cut your overhead for housing—one of the biggest fixed costs in many people's budgets—in other ways, from holding off on renovations to renting out a spare room. One entrepreneur I know sold his house in midlife and moved into a rental because he was so intent on starting a business. And in case you're wondering how the Gohs have any money left for a startup after paying doctors' bills, Singapore's national medical insurance system has protected them from the high medical costs that many patients in the United States face.

The Gohs are just getting started in their business, but they think like million-dollar entrepreneurs. Rather than looking at one-person businesses as startups that have failed to scale, they see this as a new career option that can free them to live exactly the way they want. And more important, they haven't gotten stuck in the idea phase. They are acting on their dreams—now—because they are committed to their idea. As Peter Johnson, founder and CEO of the freelancer management platform Kalo, put it, "There are so many people in big companies that procrastinate. They end up being forty years old and not doing it." That procrastination can lead to a lot of regrets—the kind that entrepreneurs like the Gohs don't have.

IDENTIFY PASSION AND USER VALUE

Each entrepreneur's goals will be unique to them. Ben and Camille Arneberg, a married couple, who live in Austin, Texas, decided they wanted to hit a very concrete goal—$1 million in revenue—when they started their upscale housewares business, Willow & Everett, in 2015. Keeping that goal in mind helped them push through challenges that might have otherwise derailed them.

When they started Willow & Everett, they were just twenty-five, and neither had any experience in retail. Ben had studied computer science at the US Air Force Academy and earned a master's degree in computer engineering at Northeastern University, becoming an engineer and program manager. Camille, who earned her master's in public relations, with a focus on nonprofits and sustainability, tried working in the corporate sustainability field but ultimately wanted a noncorporate lifestyle. She started a wedding photography business after graduate school, and over the following three years that morphed into an often full-time venture.

The duo share an interest in an active lifestyle. Ben was on an Air Force parachute team, and Camille is a certified personal trainer. They had once attempted selling compression sleeves (a runners' accessory) on the internet, hoping to turn their interest in running into a business. Although they were excited about the product, customers weren't—and the business didn't do well. "The product wasn't unique enough or desirable enough with the audience to resonate," Ben notes.

Rather than give up, the couple began brainstorming about other types of products they would enjoy selling. **They asked themselves two key questions: What are we passionate about? How can**

we deliver value to people? Camille and Ben, who love entertaining, realized they would enjoy selling products that help people host. Both really enjoy inviting people over and coming up with ideas for new cocktails or a fancy coffee they could serve, so they felt they would be comfortable building a community around that. That was not the case for some of their other interests. "There are certain hobbies I have that are deeply personal," explains Camille. "I love painting, and it is restoring for me, but it's not something I feel passionate about encouraging other people to do. It's something I like to do for myself."

They soon began researching products they could sell, looking for those that fit into a gap they saw in the marketplace — "that sweet spot of products that are high-quality, look great, and don't break the bank," says Ben. To identify these products, they searched the giant trade marketplace Alibaba.com for ideas and later began working with a sourcing agent who is on the ground in China. To find the right sourcing agent, they found five candidates on a freelance marketplace and worked with each of them for a paid trial period. Ultimately, they picked the sourcing agent they were most impressed with. They selected products like a set of two copper mugs and a shot glass that they currently sell to retail customers on their site for $36.99.

To obtain the products, they partner with a private label manufacturer they found in India. "We brand the products they already sell," says Camille. "Sometimes, we'll tweak the designs." This approach eliminates middlemen, allowing the Arnebergs to purchase their wares at prices that are less than wholesale.

HOW MUCH INVESTMENT CAN YOU RISK?

The Arnebergs had to stock up on inventory to launch their store. They invested about $5,000, raising some of it from friends and family. That's not a tiny amount of money to a couple just starting out, but they told themselves it could change their lives.

The Arnebergs looked at their startup costs as investment in their own education. "You pay thousands of dollars for a college course," Ben says. "We said, 'Let's spend five thousand dollars. We're going to learn a lot. Even if it all goes down the tube, that experience will be invaluable.'"

After researching their options, the Arnebergs decided to sell their wares through a giant e-commerce retailer, which restricts sales to the e-tailer's and Arnebergs' sites. It took a leap of faith to believe the giant platform would give them the exposure they needed. It paid off. "We've integrated well and know their team," says Ben. "They've helped us to sell our brand story."

One key part of that story is the company's focus on serving the community. The retail platform featured the business in a video on giving back for the holidays that helped raise the profile of the company, which donates 10% of its profits to nonprofits.

As the Arnebergs grew their store, they expanded it to about eighteen products, but it took some trial and error to find the ones that would sell. "We've learned that for every five products you launch, you will have maybe one or two big wins, and probably a failure or two," says Ben. "[Now] we expect to have some failures every time we launch products."

Picking the wrong product doesn't mean they lose all of their investment in it. When a product proves to be a dud, they sell it at a discount.

To stock up on products that are hot sellers, they have tapped revenue from Camille's photography business, and they participate in an internal lending program at the giant retailer, borrowing money that is paid back through their revenue at about 12% interest. They qualified for the program after they had logged a year on the retailer's platform. The lending program enabled them to triple their revenue in the span of a year. "We asked them for a couple of hundred thousand dollars so we could add new products," says Camille. "We were able to add six new products in a pretty short time frame." Having access to this financing also enabled them to keep up with demand when it was high. "In the beginning, when we were confined by capital, we would 'stock out' of our products," Camille recalls.

To stay focused on the big-picture decisions that grow their revenue, the Arnebergs don't try to do everything themselves. That means, for instance, outsourcing photography and customer service for the site. "We're just orchestrating it all, rather than implementing it," says Ben.

One area where they really save time through this approach is order fulfillment. When they ordered the first five hundred copper mugs and the delivery swamped their small condo, they decided they would never do that again. Now they rely on an outside fulfillment service run by the giant retail platform to process all of the orders. There is a cost for this, but, says Ben, "We never see anything. [The service] handles everything—fulfillment, labeling, everything you can imagine."

"That's why we've been able to stay lean," says Camille. "A lot of the normal components of an online business are removed."

As a result of all of these efforts, the couple hit the $1 million revenue mark in April 2016, one year and four days after their launch, and have since grown their revenue to more than $5 million. Around Thanksgiving of 2016, just before the December holiday rush, they hired a domestic marketing manager, who works remotely on a part-time basis, to help them. With their site humming, Ben and Camille Arneberg are hoping to live their dream of having more time for sports and fitness, visiting family and friends, and traveling.

GET CLEAR ON WHAT MATTERS

So how can you figure out what you really want out of work and whether you will be able to find it in a high-revenue solo business? Many million-dollar, one-person entrepreneurs have asked themselves what they wanted to bring into their life. Is it more time? More money? Both? A source of income that enables work from any location or at any time? A more healthful lifestyle? A creative outlet? A way to connect with people with shared passions? A means to change the world for the better? A business that can be run while young kids are in the room? A way to work in which a health problem or disability isn't an obstacle?

If asking these questions seems impractical, it's not surprising. The world of traditional work does not encourage you to think in a holistic way about your life. Many companies were built on systems that require people to behave in uniform, predictable ways so the owners could efficiently scale their operations and maximize their profits. Their punch-clock model has typically required workers to compartmentalize their home life and work life. If you want to do things in a way that suits you better, you won't fit in. Bumping up against the limitations of traditional jobs can make you feel that the way you want to work—and live—is somehow wrong. In reality, it's just inconvenient for the owners of companies who hope to maximize their own profits and those of their shareholders.

But just as mainstream medicine is moving away from relying on treatment that works for the "average" patient in favor of an individualized approach that takes into account our genetic makeup, the world of work is changing, too. Big corporations are moving away from rote ways of working in order to stay competitive with innovative startups; they realize that adopting more fluid and customized ways of working makes good business sense. Some companies are even parking entire departments in coworking spaces to spark their teams' creativity. That approach has made traditional jobs more appealing for many people, but not for everyone. If you want to work in a highly individualized way that suits you uniquely—and truly reap the profits of your labor—starting a business will give you more freedom to do that. **Just because the type of business you want to run or the way you want to work hasn't been invented yet, doesn't mean you can't be the one to do things differently.**

CONSIDER THE POSSIBILITIES

We all have subjects we geek out on. Mine is the US Census Bureau's annual statistics on nonemployer businesses. Every May, I check the Census's website for the release of the data, so I can track and report on the growth in the number of six-figure and seven-figure businesses. These businesses are one of the most exciting indicators of what work will look like in the future.

But the data doesn't go into full detail about what these businesses do. That's by design. To protect the individual owners' privacy, the government won't reveal their identity. It will tell you only what industrial category—such as retail—the businesses fall into, and enable you to slice and dice the data a bit to figure out segments (for example, approximately how many of the retailers are in e-commerce). That's about as detailed as the information gets.

To see if I could find out more, I began asking readers of my published articles to contact me if they ran million-dollar non-employer firms. Now, every few weeks, I hear from another one of these businesses or someone who knows an entrepreneur who fits the bill.

From doing these interviews, I identified the six categories of businesses that are best for creating million-dollar, one-person businesses; as listed in the introduction, these are e-commerce, manufacturing, informational content creation, professional services/creative businesses, personal services, and real estate. There probably are some others that I haven't yet discovered—or that you or other readers will go on to invent—but this list will help get you thinking about the possibilities.

E-COMMERCE

Running an e-commerce store is one of the most accessible ways to create a high-revenue, one-person business, thanks to inexpensive technologies that make it possible to put up a shop in one day. Yes, there is competition from giant e-commerce stores that can offer very low prices, but many ultra-lean online stores—often run by the owners from home—are thriving. Consider this: eCommerceFuel, an invitation-only community for owners and managers of e-commerce stores with at least $250,000 in revenue, has grown in the past five years to one thousand members whose average sales are $750,000. **"The key to success [in e-commerce] is building a reputation as a curator of a certain type of highly specialized product and creating a community of aficionados with a unique consciousness"**, says David Fairley, founder and president of Website Properties, an internet business broker based in Yelm, Washington. Says Fairley, "That's the way you avoid cutthroat pricing competition and dilution of your profitability—[by] establishing a brand no one else has."

It starts with finding a product that you're really interested in—whether that's funky ski caps or a certain type of electronic gadget—since you're going to spend a lot of time thinking about it. "The average person can be successful pretty easily by creating something very niche oriented," says Fairley. "The more niche-y, the better." Fairley has frontline experience. He has run and sold his own internet stores, including Hammocks.com, which was acquired by the large internet retailer Hayneedle.

HOW NICHE CAN YOU GO?

David Fairley has helped clients sell successful internet stores that market:

Origami materials (selling price: low seven figures)

Gumballs (selling price: seven figures)

Sleep masks (selling price: seven figures)

Muck boots (selling price: six figures)

Fairy figurines (selling price: six figures)

Decorative mailbox flags (selling price: mid six figures)

Pepper spray (selling price: six figures)

Fireplace screens (selling price: six figures)

"Who would have thought muck boots would be a six-figure business?" says Fairley. That said, you don't need to find a weird or unusual niche. "A lot of times these ideas come from what you are doing in your own life." In some cases, internet entrepreneurs have realized there are a limited number of interesting offerings in a particular category of product and decide to curate what's out there. "Suddenly they have a business," he says.

That is what happened to Boris Vaisman, thirty, and his brother Albert, twenty-four, who run the internet retailer Soxy.com, a Toronto-based e-commerce business that earned seven-figure revenue and turned a profit in its first year by liberating men from personality-stifling office dress codes. They ship uniquely patterned, high-quality socks to customers' mailboxes each month through a subscription service and also sell socks to nonsubscribers by the single pair. "It's really hard for men to get noticed," says Boris. "There's no better way than a funky, bold pair of socks."

The Vaisman brothers started out running an online retail store that carried items for a man's entire wardrobe. Their original vision was to help men look good without spending a ton of money. Then, about two years into it, they had an epiphany while studying their sales data.

"We noticed a large majority of the orders included the fun, patterned socks we were selling," says Albert. "We didn't understand why. We literally consulted with dozens of customers and learned men are extremely limited at work when it comes to standing out and expressing themselves in fashion. They're always wearing the same old suit. Guys would have sock standoffs. Every day of the week they would wear different patterns of socks. It would be a fun way to express themselves. From there on, we changed the business and decided to focus just on socks. We wanted to focus our energy on the best experience of providing socks to guys."

Changing course to achieve better product-market fit required a radical shift in mindset and letting go of their early preconceptions. "Many of us fabricate an idea for a business," says Boris. "We fall in love with it emotionally. Our mind has a risk-free way of painting an idea: It's going to succeed."

But after really listening to their customers, they could not deny that the initial picture they had painted did not reflect their customers' desires. While the brothers had gathered a variety of products they thought were great, customers' comments and their sales figures told a different story. "What they were really interested in were funky, bold socks," says Boris. That required them to make a conscious decision. "We decided to focus on what the customer wanted and not just what we wanted to sell."

Reacting to what the market was telling them has required them to paint a new picture in their minds. That wasn't easy, but they knew they had to do it to remain profitable and create a sustainable business.

Listening to their customers paid off. By relying on outsourcing and contract help to expand, and eventually hiring five employees so they didn't have to work late into the night to keep up with demand, the brothers live the lifestyle they sought when they started Soxy.com and continued to grow their revenue. Though taking on traditional employees did not make sense for them in the beginning, when they needed to keep overhead down, they had reached the point where hiring help was an important investment in their personal freedom. E-commerce is a highly competitive, very time-sensitive business, and to get a rapidly growing number of orders out the door on time without constant stress, they needed to put people on payroll. Fortunately, keeping their costs down for as long as possible gave them the financial freedom to do this.

Some entrepreneurs will come to similar crossroads; others will find they never have to add employees to achieve their goals. What is important is to recognize that businesses are not static and to make the choices that allow yours to run smoothly so you can live the way you want. "For us," says Boris, "it's all about building a business that provides the opportunity to travel, explore, and live remotely."

TEST IT

Once you have an idea that gets you excited, it's important to test it on a small scale before sinking a lot of money into it. "You can set up a website for yourself very cheaply and have someone else do it for you," says David Fairley. "You can test ideas now very inexpensively." He recommends using WordPress or Shopify to set up a basic store with e-commerce functionality. "If it takes off, you can expand from there and continue to grow it."

You may not even need to open your own site to run a test. Fairley explains, "Many entrepreneurs start by selling an item on Amazon Marketplace before they set up their own website or arrange to sell their products on daily deal sites, such as Groupon. There are lots of companies that wholesale their products and will do drop-shipping for you so you don't have to buy inventory up front until you have a sale." He recommends starting with a search for wholesale products or drop-shipping companies.

If you decide to target consumers, you will probably need to invest in some pay-per-click ads to attract shoppers to your store. "Google and Facebook are great places to start selling," Fairley says. By using their pay-per-click ads, you can test the interest level in your products quickly. If no one shows up, you can always try again with a different project.

SHORTCUT THE LEARNING CURVE

In any new business, there's a learning curve. To get to $1 million in revenue, many entrepreneurs take a shortcut: they start a business in an area they already know well, whether in a field they had worked in or a hobby or other personal pursuit. That helps them avoid rookie mistakes and scale revenue quickly. **As you consider the options in front of you, it pays to tap into expertise you've already built.**

That's especially true in e-commerce, where an insider's knowledge of your marketplace and products can give you an amazing competitive edge. For instance, Allen Walton, twenty-nine, leveraged his past experience working in a security camera store to build SpyGuy, an online store that broke $1 million in revenue its first year. Frustrated with the world of traditional jobs and a paycheck that didn't reflect the work he put in, he decided to work for himself. Armed with just $1,000 he'd saved, he took his own spy camera shop live three years ago.

Walton soon discovered he had something many entrepreneurs crave: an unfair competitive advantage. During the time he spent selling cameras and other gadgets to consumers who came to the store and later, running an online store for another entrepreneur, he had essentially earned a master's degree in picking the right inventory. "I know exactly what products they want and what they are using them for," he said. In the first twelve months, he created a store that sold about a hundred products he was confident his customers would want, sinking about $10,000 into inventory.

Thanks to his Google Adwords campaigns, Walton's store picked up customers quickly. With customers ranging from the US Army to parents who want to make sure children with autism are not being abused by caregivers, the store is thriving. Not long after the one-year mark, demand had gotten so high that he hired an employee to handle customer service, then hired two more. He'd brought in $1.9 million in annual revenue last year, and he has no intention of slowing down.

CONSIDER THE
BUSINESS-TO-BUSINESS MARKET

You don't necessarily need to sell your products to consumers. Business-to-business customers can be attractive, too, and allow you a very different business model. Harry Ein, thirty-nine, brings in $3.5 to $4 million a year in revenue at Perfection Promo, a business that combines e-commerce with other sales methods, offering swag, such as T-shirts silk-screened with a company's name, from his garage in Walnut Creek, California. His clients include a number of professional sports organizations. One recent week, he provided eighteen thousand T-shirts in a game-day giveaway. He also serves merchants, such as a fifty-store coffee chain where he provides the retail merchandise, the gift shop of a Las Vegas hotel, and companies that, for instance, want to outfit their employees in hoodies emblazoned with their logo.

What enables Ein to pull it off is outsourcing work, including filling orders, which are handled by iPROMOTEu in Wayland, Massachusetts. They work out terms with his vendors, pay deposits, and collect money from his customers, while he focuses on sales and growing the company. As his company has grown to the point where it sometimes processes several hundred orders a week, he has arranged to have an outside sales assistant at iPROMOTEu help him. He essentially pays half of the assistant's salary in the form of distributions that iPROMOTEu takes from his commissions as an independent sales representative. "That makes it seamless for me," says Ein. "I don't have to deal with payroll."

Even though he outsources, Ein occasionally works on weekends, as he did when a client couldn't locate a shipment of three thousand T-shirts for a conference that was taking place in three days. "It's not like I'm working Monday to Friday, nine to five, and I'm not going to answer a phone call or email," says Ein. He doesn't mind working outside of traditional business hours, given the freedom it brings him. Ein coaches T-ball and has plenty of time to take his son to swimming and the park. "I love working from home, being able to service my clients from here, and spending time with my son," says Ein. "I'm not spending one and a half hours commuting. By saving that time, I can service my clients the best way possible, be involved with all of my son's activities, and not miss anything—while creating a business that's very successful."

Not long ago, when Ein arrived to one of his son's activities wearing a sweatshirt in the middle of the day, another parent ribbed him with, "Harry, rough day," because he looked like he hadn't been working. Ein laughed it off. He's living exactly the life he wants.

"You need to love what you do," says Ein. "I wake up and don't hate my job. I work hard, but I love it. I love the excitement. I love the projects."

THE ONE-PERSON FRANCHISE OPTION

You may be surprised to know that it is possible to break $1 million in revenue in a one-person *franchise*—a type of business typically known for requiring employees. That's what shipping industry veteran Christopher Cadigan, forty-two, did at Unishippers of Nassau County South in Oyster Bay, New York. He broke the million-dollar barrier as a one-man operation because of one very important strategic decision: outsourcing his customer service, billing, and collections to a virtual management firm in Melbourne, Florida, so he could devote his attention to shipping. "The phones and emails are answered exactly the way [they would be] if these people were sitting there next to me," Cadigan told me. He was so impressed by the virtual management firm, Right Growth Shipping, that he eventually partnered in it—and now helps other franchisees manage their businesses the same way. Meanwhile, Unishippers of Nassau County South grew to the point that he decided it made sense to hire help; he now employs five sales people.

MANUFACTURING

Thanks to new technologies, it is increasingly possible for one-person operations to manufacture products to be sold around the world. 3D printing is one way to get in on this trend, but there are other possibilities. Contracting out manufacturing to a factory is a popular way for ultra-lean businesses to mass-produce products. Sites like Maker's Row, an online marketplace that connects small businesses with factories and other resources they need to turn their ideas into products, have made it easier to source materials, fabricators, and manufacturers without getting on a plane. Free videoconferencing tools you can access from your laptop now allow you to do tasks like viewing a prototype from thousands of miles away. These trends are fueling opportunity. The US Census Bureau found there were 355,467 nonemployer establishments involved in manufacturing in 2015, up from 350,346 in 2014—despite daily headlines about the decline in US manufacturing. Among them, 29,982 brought in $100,000 to $249,999 in revenue in 2015, 9,840 generated $250,000 to $499,999, 4,530 made $500,000 to $999,999 in revenue and 91 broke $1 million.

"Now small businesses can compete and be very flexible in how they scale up or scale down their business," says Intuit's Alex Hood. **"The cost structure big businesses used to use as an advantage is breaking down."**

The million-dollar, nonemployer manufacturers I have encountered have often combined their manufacturing operations with a direct-to-consumer e-commerce store. For instance, Scott Paladini, an entrepreneur whose story you will read in the next chapter, hires a factory to make mattresses that can be compressed into small boxes and sold to customers who order them from a web store he set up inexpensively.

Rebeca Krones, thirty-eight, and her husband, Luis Zevallos, fifty-four, didn't expect to work in the honey business when they started their careers. Krones, who had studied art history at Oberlin College, was working as operations manager in an art gallery, while Zevallos, a sous chef, was employed by a restaurant in the San Francisco Bay Area when they began to think about going a different route, one that would give them more control over their time.

Krones's father, Michael Krones, owns the farm Hawaiian Queen Co. on the Big Island of Hawaii, where he produces queen bees for export, serving the agricultural sector in the United States and Canada. Through her exposure to his farm, Krones learned a lot about the honey business. She says, "Honey is a natural byproduct of his work." One day Krones noticed that her father's company was selling the honey in fifty-five-gallon drums and not maximizing profit.

The couple realized they could build a retail brand around the honey that Hawaiian Queen Co. produced. In 2005, they began to work on marketing Royal Hawaiian Honey and started selling it through an online retail site and directly to retailers on the Big Island of Hawaii.

Gradually, they found their focus: raw, certified organic honey. "There's a growing base of honey consumers in the United States that want honey that is closer to the way bees produce it," says Krones. "That's basically our niche."

Tropical Traders sells its honey at premium prices. Nonetheless, the couple has found that there is high demand. Many consumers are looking for honey they know does not contain harmful contaminants—a problem in some honey imported from China, for example.

As demand for their organic honey picked up, the couple realized they couldn't produce enough at the farm in Hawaii to keep up. Krones's father introduced them to a cooperative of beekeepers in Brazil. Soon they began selling Brazilian honey under the Bee Well brand. "That is a much larger volume of honey," says Krones. Having access to the honey has allowed them to meet more of the demand they see in the marketplace. "It's been able to catapult us into position," says Krones.

The two-person company has been able to grow to more than $1 million in revenue by outsourcing. Along the way, they have had some ups and downs related to weather conditions—a factor worth noting if you are interested in running a business tied to agriculture. In 2015, the business brought in $1.7 million in revenue. The following year, however, revenue slipped to under $1 million when a drought in Brazil prevented the couple from buying the volume of honey they desired. They got back on track and in 2017 expected to hit or exceed $1 million in revenue. "Following your dreams is never a straight path, as you can see from our sales, but we feel entirely committed to it, nonetheless," says Krones.

One thing that has enabled them to weather the unexpected is keeping their costs down. Instead of running their own packing facility, the couple hires a company known as a copacker to package the honey in compliance with rigorous food certification standards. Krones, who has worked closely with an advisor from her local Small Business Development Center to grow the business, says using the copacker represents about 16% of the cost of goods sold, a figure that varies with the size of a run, but it's worth it.

"If you bring on employees and have your own facility, there is enormous overhead involved in that," says Krones. "We looked for a way to launch the product that would maximize the ability to scale it without any of the risks."

Teaming up with the copacker has also allowed the couple to meet another goal: Enjoying time with their growing family. They have two sons. "Our goal is to be able to spend as much time with our kids as we can," says Krones, who was forty weeks pregnant with their youngest when interviewed. "Being able to outsource allows me to work from home and spend more time with them."

INFORMATIONAL CONTENT CREATION

If you've developed unique expertise in a subject that interests many people, chances are there is someone willing to pay you for it. Package it in a format you can sell online — whether through webcasts, videos, books, ebooks, seminars, or podcasts — and you can join the growing ranks of info-marketers who make money by selling information. There are info-marketers selling everything from instructions for DIY craft projects to fitness plans to original recipes.

Often the founders of these businesses started them because they were looking for information they wanted but couldn't find. Sol Orwell, for instance, started Examine.com six years ago because he had a goal many people share: he wanted to slim down. He started researching nutritional supplements that would help with that goal. "There is all of this research out there on supplementation but no organization putting it together," he observed. By selling to that unmet interest, he realized he could build a thriving business.

Not being an expert on nutrition, Orwell hired PhDs and other experts as freelance consultants on topics such as lipidology, cardiovascular disease, and public health to evaluate the research on various supplements. He also relied on the best freelancers he could find in other areas of the business. "What I've found is hiring the best makes life one hundred times easier," says Orwell. "The graphic designer we use is one hundred and fifty dollars per hour. I've sent a dozen-plus people her way."

Though that rate may sound high for a startup to pay, the gains in time saved, clarity, and quality more than justified it, Orwell found. As many entrepreneurs on tight budgets discover, professionals who have expertise at what they do often take far less time to accomplish a goal than a novice who charges a rock-bottom hourly rate. And you'll probably find that you spend less time on revisions when working with people who really know what they are doing. They will often be able to come up with solutions to challenges that may not be on the radar of an inexperienced competitor, by virtue of having solved them for other clients. In the end, your bill from a top pro may end up being lower than one from a rookie who you think will save you money.

Four years ago, Examine.com released its first product: a mega-sized ebook, *The Supplement Goals Reference Guide*, which collects and synthesizes reams of research on supplementation. Orwell sells the guide for $49 through a custom site he put up and has generated about $200,000 in sales.

Although the reference guide did well, when Orwell asked for feedback from customers, he says he heard: "I love your stuff, but it's too nerdy. I can't read it—or my mom can't." That led Examine.com to create a series of sixteen shorter Stack Guides offering more streamlined information about supplements for laypeople. "After that we had serious revenue," says Orwell.

Generating that money helped him reinvest in the business. "I was able to bring in a lot of contractors," Orwell says. "We were able to build this entire team of subject matter experts we can turn to whenever we need advice on a particular topic."

Recently, Examine.com released a new product: its *Research Digest*, a twice-a-month newsletter aimed at professionals. For $30 a month, subscribers find out about the latest nutrition studies. None of Orwell's products are printed, keeping his investment in creating them low.

To promote his wares, Orwell uses email lists he has built up over the years, which keeps his marketing overhead down. "If people are willing to give you their email address, which they treasure, they are willing to listen to your message," he says.

Nick Shaw, twenty-nine, a competitive powerlifter and bodybuilder, has taken a similar approach to info-marketing at Renaissance Periodization, a training and diet services company for athletes and fitness enthusiasts, which was a one-man, seven-figure business until late 2015, when he got so busy that he recruited his wife to help him. Working from his home in Charlotte, North Carolina, he has hired a team of more than twenty PhDs and registered dieticians as consultants to help him develop high-quality products. "Our advantage is our knowledge," says Shaw. "If you just do this on your own, you don't really have a whole lot more to offer than anyone else who already does it."

Shaw has scaled his revenue by thinking beyond one-on-one services. Having earned a bachelor's degree in sports management, he originally built his startup around diet coaching for athletes, starting with bodybuilders—a market he knew from his personal experience in the sport. However, he quickly saw that there was a limit to how much coaching he could do personally and through the consultants he hired. "How do you scale diet coaching?" he kept asking himself. As a father of two, he didn't want to spend every waking hour at work in order to grow his revenue.

Eventually, Shaw came up with an answer. Working with exercise physiology consultant Mike Israetel—an assistant professor of instruction in kinesiology at Temple University who helped him cofound the business—he developed prebuilt diets that would allow customers to access his advice without working with him directly. The diets can be customized according to someone's gender, weight, and goals. Customers order the diets through his website. The most popular coaching offering, the 3-Month Diet Plan, goes for $575, and customers who add training to the plan pay $750. The training and coaching is done by email or via social media.

Like Orwell, Shaw didn't rely on one product alone. The diet templates, now his most popular products, are designed to help someone either lose or gain weight in a concentrated period of time. They go for about $100, depending on the plan. "Working with templates, the scalability is limitless," says Shaw. "The templates reach tens of thousands of people." Shaw also sells several ebooks for about $30 each.

As Renaissance Periodization took off, it was hard for Shaw to keep up with sending out his products himself, so he had to find ways to run his operations more efficiently. He began relying on Infusionsoft, a customer relationship management software, to manage communications with customers and mailings. "We were able to automate everything on our website," he says. That made the difference between being able to serve several hundred customers and working with tens of thousands worldwide.

Not sure what type of information you have the expertise to market? If you have a near-obsessive passion for a particular interest or pursuit in your own life, you are positioned to build a business around it. Wondering what type of information actually sells? For starters, look through the offerings at ClickBank, an internet retailer that sells thousands of digital products, to get a sense of the type of content that sells well. Also check out the lists of best sellers on online bookstores and existing high-traffic blogs in your niche (they'll come up highest in an internet search) for ideas on what people with similar interests respond to. Then figure out a way to add something new to the conversation.

Daniel Faggella, twenty-nine, a black belt in Brazilian jiu-jitsu, experimented with ways to make money from his passion for martial arts until he found one that was lucrative enough to turn into a profitable seven-figure business—and sold it for more than $1 million. The business brought in $210,000 for the month just before it was acquired, he says. The subscription-based e-commerce site he created, Science of Skill, sells online fitness, self-defense, and self-protection curricula and products to students around the world.

Faggella did not set out to be an internet entrepreneur. He studied cognitive science during graduate school. "That's the stuff I'm super-duper passionate about," he says. "However, I can't just pursue that like I'm on sabbatical and have a rich uncle."

Faggella earned enough to pay for graduate school by running a small martial arts gym he owned when he was in his early twenties but had sold by the time he was twenty-five, when he decided to move on to an e-commerce business. He was most passionate about fighting and competing, and though the gym was profitable, it was not easily scalable. "In a martial arts facility, such as the one I had, to get to one million dollars in revenue is very, very difficult without employees," he says. "I would need multiple front desk staff, multiple instructors."

After reading a book called *Scaling Up* (Rockefeller Habits 2.0, 2014) by Verne Harnish (on which I, coincidentally, collaborated), Faggella changed course and set his sights on launching a scalable, location-independent business that would ultimately generate enough money for him to fund a third business in which he could pursue his interest in cognitive science. Initially, at Science of Skill, he started out selling courses in martial arts online. That seemed like a natural fit. Among martial artists, Faggella, who has a slight build, has achieved some renown for a championship fight in which he creamed a much larger competitor. Faggella discovered that others found his success on the mat inspiring—and instructive. "A lot of my matches against bigger guys ended up being very interesting for people online," he says. Traffic on the site grew steadily, as martial arts aficionados flocked.

Nonetheless, Faggella soon realized there were limits to this idea. There were only so many videos he could offer of himself before he ran out of material. He began looking for other martial arts experts who aired videos of their own fighting techniques on YouTube channels and communities on Facebook—but were not necessarily making money from it—to contribute content. Although many martial arts pros offer private lessons, he says, "Most are on the verge of living with their mother. I used to be one of them."

Faggella soon developed partnerships with more than a dozen instructors, both in the United States (Texas) and overseas (Norway, Sweden), who developed online courses that he sold on his site. All were glad to get more exposure than they were getting on their own websites and social media pages.

Beyond the exposure the instructors got through Science of Skill, Faggella paid them twice what they would receive for a private lesson for each video. So, for instance, a martial arts pro who charged $100 an hour received $200 for one hour of video footage.

But even selling a wider variety of martial arts content had its limitations. What allowed Faggella to make the leap from six-figure to seven-figure revenue was reaching a larger audience. "The big growth for us came when we left the martial arts world or Brazilian jiu-jitsu world, which is a very small, dark corner of the internet," says Faggella. "We expanded from there into a much broader market of self-protection and self-reliance—people interested in preventing home break-ins, getting firearms training, or learning basic self-defense techniques."

When Faggella sold the business, it was generating revenue from a range of products. One of the biggest ones was an ongoing curriculum for self-defense and martial arts techniques. Faggella had also added a variety of self-defense equipment, such as martial arts knives, and DVD programs. He grew the business to its seven-figure revenue by relying on the help of four loyal contractors to help with tasks such as copywriting and web support.

Even better, Science of Skill allowed Faggella to pursue his other passion. He had simultaneously run another business called Tech Emergence, a San Francisco media and market research firm focused on artificial intelligence. "I never wanted to do stuff I wasn't actually very interested in," says Faggella. Now, with the proceeds of the sale of Science of Skill, he will have a chance to do a deep dive into artificial intelligence.

PROFESSIONAL SERVICES

Scaling revenue at a service business—whether it is a law firm, graphic design shop, or marketing agency—is notoriously difficult. Service professionals' income is usually limited by how many hours they can put in. But exceptions exist. **Owners of one-person professional services businesses who want to break $1 million in revenue often do so in two ways: (1) by making creative use of automation, outsourcing, and help from independent contractors, or (2) by charging higher prices than their competitors.**

Let's look at the first approach. When Pamela Grossman suffered a debilitating panic attack on the way to her job at an ad agency nearly two decades ago, the Atlanta-based multimedia producer soon learned she was suffering from a serious panic disorder. She embarked on years of treatment and learning to manage her condition, which made it difficult to leave her house. She could have gone on disability, but she was determined to reinvent herself and did so by starting her own business, In The Present, a boutique marketing and production studio. "I love to work," she told me. "I can't *not* work."

In The Present does logo design, brand building, marketing and promotional programs, social media marketing, and video production for clients. To go after the kinds of big jobs she had handled in her corporate career, Grossman built a network of contractors around the globe, paying very competitive rates to get the best talent. She uses tools such as WhatsApp, the design tool Figma, GoToMeeting, and Skype to work collaboratively with both her talent pool and her clients, and she has gained a competitive edge by having freelancers in different time zones working around the clock, so she can offer clients speedy turnarounds. Meanwhile, working with a service dog—a labradoodle named Milo—has helped her make tremendous progress on managing her condition. Grossman's one-woman business brings in upward of $2 million per year.

Some entrepreneurs scale professional services firms, such as consultancies, by increasing their hourly rates or retainers as they build a track record of success. Another way to do this is by putting together a package of services or a training program for premium prices and selling them to prospects who can afford them. This approach can work in tandem with other approaches, such as building a network of reliable contractors.

HOW TO RAISE YOUR PROFESSIONAL SERVICES PRICES

Raising your prices can take courage, but often it's the only way to grow revenue in a service business. Fortunately, it is possible to do it without losing your clients, as many entrepreneurs have found. Here's how.

Figure out where you're making a profit. When you first start a business, it may be worthwhile to take on clients that are not very profitable to get some cash flowing into the business and build momentum. Taking on a well-known client you can mention in your marketing or an influential client who is likely to refer new business your way, even at slightly less than you want to charge, can help you get established—even if you're barely breaking even on the projects.

But after you have been in business a while, it doesn't make sense to keep working with unprofitable clients. You will not generate enough money to cover your overhead or reinvest in the business. By tallying up the money you're bringing in from each client every quarter and looking at the time and money you're investing to complete the client's projects, you'll be able to determine if you are breaking even or turning a profit. If you aren't, you may be better off either raising prices or replacing the client with one that is more profitable.

Get a sense of market rates. In consumer product businesses, it is easy to figure out what prices the market will bear because your competitors probably advertise them online or publish them on their websites. In a professional services business, you will probably have to take a different approach. Joining a trade organization that offers market reports on how much independent professionals in your field are charging can be a good investment. In my own business, spending $200 per year to belong to such a group has paid for itself many times over. If you can't find a group like this, talking with friendly competitors in the same geographic area can be a good way to find out what the common rates are for a particular service. Are most of them charging more than you do? Then it's probably time to consider a rate increase.

Calculate the return on your client's investment. Clients probably will not mind paying you more if you're doing a great job and you can show them how hiring you more than pays for itself. Look for objective ways to quantify the financial gains you have brought a client before approaching them with a rate hike. For instance, if you coached a client's sales team for six months, and now sales have tripled, you can easily make a strong case for paying you more.

The value you provide doesn't necessarily have to translate directly into dollars. For instance, if you are a public speaking coach and your client has, as a result of your coaching, been invited to speak at better venues or to deliver speeches more often, that may have value, too, even if the client isn't getting paid to speak yet.

Consider how you will raise your rates. The simplest way to raise rates is to charge more for the same service, but that isn't the only way. Some business owners will repackage the services they offer so that, for instance, clients can no longer obtain a particular service on an à la carte basis and must purchase a package that builds in pricing at premium rates. For more ideas, look at how other players in your niche are packaging their services.

Test the waters. Before raising prices across the board, try upping your rates with one of your friendlier clients first, or initiate the rate increase with new clients only. If you get pushback, you may need to refine your approach. It could be that clients and prospects are willing to pay more, but not as much as you are asking. Consider how you will deal with that possibility ahead of time. While you don't want to work at a financial loss, you don't want to drive away all of your clients by raising prices too quickly, either. It could be that six months from now your value will be much more clear, making it far easier to increase your prices without resistance. Having a diversity of clients, rather than a concentration of business with just one or two, gives you some protection against the possibility that a major account will dry up suddenly if you decide you must raise rates.

Make sure you get paid. Regardless of what you charge, you will not have a business if you don't get paid. Make sending out invoices part of your weekly routine, and follow up on them if clients don't pay you on time. Asking for deposits on projects and progress payments is customary in many professional services firms, so don't be afraid to ask clients for terms like these. Some trade and industry associations will even provide you with sample contracts. If prospective customers balk at such an arrangement, ask yourself how likely they will be to pay you later.

In industries where deposits and progress payments are not common, don't do more work for any client before getting a payment than you can afford to lose if they default. There is nothing wrong with saying to a late-paying client who wants to charge ahead with more work, "I'm a one-person business and am not in a position to finance projects for my clients. Is it possible to get caught up on the last invoice before moving ahead?" Reasonable clients will understand that. If a client can't pay you $1,000 owed now, it's not likely he or she will be able to pay you for an additional $10,000 worth of work. And one of the most unpleasant tasks of the one-person business is having to pursue a client for unpaid invoices.

PERSONAL SERVICES

Whether they offer dog walking or diet coaching, personal services firms have the same limitations as professional services firms. **When you offer personal services, time is the commodity you are selling. But that doesn't mean you can't scale your revenue if you think creatively.**

Joey Healy, twenty-nine, is a prime example. The New York City entrepreneur runs an eyebrow styling business called the Joey Healy Eyebrow Studio. He started the business by traveling on foot to the apartments of well-heeled Manhattanites to style their brows. While his customers had the means to pay him well—actresses such as Kyra Sedgewick have been clients—there was only so much he could charge for a styling, and his business model, built on traveling to clients' locations, was not particularly efficient. He soon found himself working very long hours as he tried to grow the business. "I would book my day from 9 a.m. to 9 p.m. on Park Avenue," he told me when we first spoke; he was then twenty-seven.

Healy eventually decided to open a private studio, where he charged $115 for a brow styling, and clients came to him. That made a difference, but his big breakthrough came when he negotiated a profit-sharing arrangement with a spa chain with four New York locations; he trained the chain's stylists to use his methodology. Between the money he brought in from the spa chain and from selling his own line of brow makeup—made through an outsourced manufacturer—Healy broke $1 million a year without hiring any employees.

Healy is an example of how growing an ultra-lean business to seven-figure revenue can open unexpected opportunities. He could have easily kept his operation very small, like many freelancers in the beauty and fashion industries, simply by limiting the number of customers he served. Not long after he broke $1 million, however, he made the decision to keep growing the business. It had begun to take off so quickly that he hired an assistant to handle tasks such as filling web and wholesale orders, creating marketing newsletters, and scheduling. He soon moved his private studio to a much larger, one-thousand-square-foot ground level location in prime real estate at University Place in

Manhattan, where it has been based since late 2015. "This was a big go-big-or-go-home moment for me," he says. His rent was six time higher than in his previous location. To make the most of his investment, he expanded his current staff to include five other people—a process that was not without bumps. "Many came and went before we got the ideal staff combination down," he told me.

Although his costs rose substantially, Healy said his business has remained profitable every single month. "The brow business is a money machine, and I'm happy to have scaled my business so it has the potential to grow further," he says. "Especially since I have retained 100 percent of our business, I now have a model that can attract investors who can replicate our operation." He is also relieved that he no longer has to worry that if he goes skiing, he might break his wrist and render himself unable to see clients. "Now having a space that is open seven days a week with a diverse staff of service providers and support administration, I can take a mental break and know that my one-time little operation has a life of its own and a future ahead of it."

There are many other types of ultra-lean personal services businesses that solo entrepreneurs are scaling. For instance, since 1997, Debra Cohen, forty-nine, has run what has become a million-dollar business from her home in Hewlett, New York, helping consumers find home improvement contractors they can trust. Consumers can use her Homeowner Referral Network for free, but contractors pay a commission on jobs when they complete them. Though the Homeowner Referral Network has no employees other than Cohen, she gets all of the help she needs from hiring contractors as her virtual assistant, webmaster, and IT pro. "That's probably my biggest cost saver," she notes.

As Nick Shaw found, even a one-man fitness training business can scale its revenues. But his approach to scaling the business—through content sales—isn't the only one. Dan Mezheritsky, whom we met in chapter 1 (page 13), took a very different approach in founding his in-home personal training franchise, Fitness on the Go, based in Vancouver, British Columbia. He relies on contractors to do the training.

As a junior national champion decathlete in Canada, Mezheritsky tore his hamstring at age twenty after competing in the Canadian Olympic trials and continuing to train. "Having to go through a lot of rehab, I learned a lot about the body, but after a tear like that, it wasn't really possible to compete," he says. Mezheritsky decided to become a personal trainer but wanted to accomplish more than he could as a solo operator.

In 2005, he started Fitness on the Go in Vancouver, hiring other personal trainers as traditional employees. Within the first three years he sold $1.5 million worth of training.

But working with the employees was frustrating. He didn't find them to be particularly motivated to help him grow the business. "The personal trainers would build a very good relationship with the customer," says Mezheritsky. "What that led to was the personal trainer or customer proposing a side deal. If the trainer was being paid twenty dollars, and a customer was paying sixty, they would agree to forty, cut Fitness on the Go out of the equation, and work on their own."

Sometimes trainers were unprofessional in other ways. One trainer asked to use the washroom at a customer's house—and took a shower. Mezheritsky got so frustrated that he almost gave up. Then he asked himself why he was sticking to a business model built on hiring employees. The real estate industry, he noticed, was operating successfully with a different approach — one in which a parent company would license brokerages to independent owners.

Mezheritsky decided to start over, using a franchise/licensing model. He began licensing the right to use the company's brand name to individual trainers. They liked being part of a brand that handles things like advertising and social media and had built both strong relationships with personal training schools and certification bodies in its industry, and a track record of delivering a consistent experience that its fans really like — value that, even in a relatively young business, he was able to deliver effectively. "A lot of personal trainers would love to be entrepreneurs," he says. The company sets prices and trainers receive about 91% of their clients' fees. And they pay Fitness on the Go $400 a month, for which they receive services, including business management help, continuing education, and back-end infrastructure support. The business has thirteen franchise partners in Canada, who recruit and manage trainers in their area.

Mezheritsky's model works. The business has grown to the point that it has about 180 personal trainers in Canada and has broken $4 million in system-wide revenues. At his corporate headquarters, where he is still the only worker, he brings in more than $1 million, with about 25% profit. He is expanding into the United States next.

Mezheritsky's secret to growing the business without formal employees is customized software that automates many functions. The software, which cost him about $25,000 to get up and running, enables clients to log into the company's computer system and see the homework that their trainers have assigned, among other functions. But more important, he says, is the fact that it is a full education platform for trainers, a customer relationship management system that allows them to keep in touch with clients, a billing system, and home to a client rewards program — simplifying many aspects of business for the trainers. The system, in which he has gradually invested about $250,000 in total, is so important to the business that he pays a developer $1,000 a month to keep editing it. "We've licensed it to other companies," he says. "As soon as they see it, they want it."

Looking back at his business journey, Mezheritsky realizes that under the traditional model of hiring employees, turning a profit meant creating a "negative lifestyle" for employees. He couldn't pay them a salary that would motivate them or get them invested in the company's success. "Maybe the top trainer was making seventy-five thousand dollars a year," he says. As a result, employees were showing up just to collect a paycheck.

In his new model, his interests and those of his trainers are aligned. Because he makes money from the recurring fees the trainers pay him, he is highly incentivized to help them succeed and keep them part of his brand. And they are extremely motivated to grow their businesses because they are the ones who make more money when they do.

"Not only are we attracting people I could never have attracted as employees, but they're paying us four hundred dollars a month to provide those services for them," he says. "They are making about sixty thousand dollars. And the overall vibe of the business is better. Everyone is here because they want to be. That's a good goal to aim for in a personal service business, where you and your team need to be primed to keep your customers happy.

THE POWER OF YOUR BRAND

In a one-person business, you are not realistically going to develop a brand with the recognition of a multinational company. That takes millions of advertising and marketing dollars.

Nonetheless, building a brand around what you sell will help you attract and keep customers by making your business memorable. This is especially important for businesses, such as internet stores, that need to distinguish themselves from big players that are better able to compete on prices. One way Camille and Ben Arneberg have managed to grow Willow & Everett so quickly is by building a strong brand as talented curators of items that appeal to home entertainers.

Factors such as the name of your business, the look and feel of your logo and website, and the fonts you use all contribute to your brand. So do the media in which you choose to communicate.

But branding goes beyond your image. Underlying any successful brand is the value it provides to customers and the consistency with which it delivers that value. Branding reflects the company's values as well—innovation, giving back to the community, high-end customer service, whatever matters to you.

In your branding, don't try to hide the fact that you are running a very small business. Many people like to do business with a company run by an identifiable person whom they can contact directly or who answers their comments posted on a website. It is part of the brand's charm.

As you grow your business, you will have many opportunities to experiment with and refine your brand and market it. Marketing guru Seth Godin's blog and books are great resources, as are David Meerman Scott's books, such as *The New Rules of Marketing and PR* (Wiley, 2017). Their ideas will help you no matter what size your business.

REAL ESTATE

If you prefer investing to traditional entrepreneurship, buying real estate can be an ideal route to building a high-revenue one-person business. Many people who start solo businesses as real estate investors work in other professions by the day, generating income they can invest in real estate. In the real estate, rental, and leasing field, in 2015 there were 2.6 million nonemployer firms. Among them, 701,790 brought in revenue from $100,000 to $999,999, and 2,555 brought in $1 million to $2.49 million annually.

Cory Binsfield, a financial advisor, is one example. Working as a financial advisor in San Francisco after college, he had an epiphany during his commute on the Golden Gate Bridge: "It was the middle of the afternoon," he says. "Traffic was so backed up I could barely move. I said, 'What am I doing here? It's beautiful, but I'm tied up in traffic.'"

Binsfield had never imagined moving back to his hometown of Duluth, Minnesota, a city of about eighty-five thousand people on the shores of Lake Superior, near Canada. Compared to San Francisco, it seemed like a small town.

But getting free from the crowding of big-city life now seemed urgent. A day after the traffic jam, he phoned his father to say he was moving back to Duluth—a decision that, unbeknownst to him, would enable him to build a million-dollar microbusiness.

While establishing his financial advisory practice in Duluth, Binsfield noticed a phenomenon that would allow him to multiply his income exponentially. Among his self-employed clients, he found that those who were in a good position to retire often had one thing in common: rental income.

"The ones who owned the building or had real estate were saying, 'Hey, I'm moving to Florida,'" he says. And he noticed that those who had been planning on selling their business but did not own property often found that their plan did not pan out because of health issues, divorce, and other unexpected events.

Shocked at how low real estate prices in Duluth were, relative to California, Binsfield decided to try real estate investing. He'd always loved old buildings with vintage hardware. "Even when I was dead broke, working in San Francisco, I used to just walk through neighborhoods and admire the architecture," he says. "It was always a passion." He went through a phase where he spent a lot of money on real estate books and courses emphasizing the "get rich quick" mindset, but gradually he realized that this wasn't how real estate investing works. "It's get rich slow," he says.

He bought his first property at age thirty-three, four years after moving back to his hometown. "If these guys can do it, I can do it, too," he told himself. On that deal and others to follow, he took the advice of a wealthy almond farmer he'd known in California, which was essentially to hack his housing. "Always make money while living in your house," the farmer had told him. Binsfield bought a triplex and moved into one unit. "For some reason, I love landlording," he says. And no one yells at him when the stock market is crashing, as they do in his financial advisory business.

Now, at age fifty-two, Binsfield owns 116 units. He owns properties from duplexes to apartment buildings and brings in more than $1 million in annual revenue. When he needs help with paperwork, he relies on the administrative assistant he hired for his financial advisory practice.

You're probably wondering how Binsfield managed to buy 116 units. The answer is by patiently working toward that goal. He didn't have a lot of money to invest at first. "I moved here dead broke after living in San Francisco," he recalls. When he calculated his net worth at the time, it was negative $45,000, he observes with a chuckle. And his financial advisory practice was growing very slowly. "I was lucky if I made $50,000 in a given year," he recalls. Though he had good credit, he found that banks were leery of lending to him because he was self-employed. To buy his first property, he negotiated financing from the seller. After that, he built enough of a track record to borrow from banks.

To reduce the risks of buying a dud property, he stuck with investing in areas he knew. "What I discovered was if you picked an area in town that was desirable and was within transportation and biking distance to work—with a lot of activity in terms of ethnic restaurants and shopping areas—you start attracting a lot more millennials and college kids," he says. "I pretty much focused on areas near the campus that weren't too high priced." In areas he did not know as well, he would often park his car and walk the streets—or skateboard around on his longboard—looking for deals. "It was skateboarding for dollars," he says.

Along the way, he used the "1% rule" to make decisions. He found that in order for a real estate investment to work out financially, the rents needed to equal at least 1% of the purchase price of the property. For instance, if the property cost him $100,000, monthly rents would need to be $1,000.

Setting clear goals—like the plan to buy ten duplexes in a decade, which he achieved in five years—kept Binsfield focused. "After that, I was like, 'Now what?' I said, 'This is kind of fun. I'll keep doing it.'" He'd achieved $1 million in net worth after steadily investing and reinvesting for eight years and $1 million in annual revenue two years ago, he says. Today he estimates his net worth at $2.5 million.

Staying local was another key to Binsfield's success. That enabled him to manage his real estate while running his other business. He could easily run out at lunchtime and do a showing if he kept his properties within his strike zone. "All of my buildings were about a mile and a half between work and my house," he says. All told, he found it took him about one hour a month to manage ten units. Once he realized how low the time commitment was, he felt empowered to buy more properties. "I thought I if I can manage ten units in an hour a month, let's bring that up to a hundred units," he says.

Another smart move was outsourcing property management. Binsfield handled light repairs himself for a while but, not being mechanically inclined, soon found a reliable contractor to tackle the work. Investing in property management software made it easier to field requests from tenants and send them off to the contractor. "I'm like the conductor of the orchestra," he says.

Becoming a landlord has opened up interesting new sidelines for Binsfield. In addition to his other pursuits, he now blogs and runs a podcast on buying rental property at the site Ten to Million (tentomillion.com) His advice for others who want to generate an income like his from real estate? Start small.

"Anyone can buy one property," he says. "Once you buy that first one, two or three years later you buy the second." You may not end up owning 116 units like he does, but if you buy in the right market, you should see a worthwhile return on your investment.

IDENTIFY WHERE YOUR PASSION MEETS MARKET DEMAND

Even if you decide to pursue a business that interests you and in which you have some expertise, those factors alone won't guarantee you a successful business. There also has to be a market for what you sell.

Rich and Vicki Fulop realized this early on. The married couple run Brooklinen, a startup in Brooklyn, New York, that sells stylish luxury bed linens online. After discovering a set of sheets on vacation that they loved—and learning that the suggested retail price was a whopping $800—they thought they saw an opportunity in the marketplace. They would sell high-quality linens with clean, minimalist designs from an online store for a much lower price than comparable sheet sets.

There was one major obstacle. At the time, neither one of them had experience in the linens business. When the Fulops, who got married in 2010, started Brooklinen, Rich, thirty-one, was an MBA student at NYU's Stern School of Business, and Vicki, thirty-two, was an account executive at a public relations agency in New York City. That meant they had to figure out how to design and manufacture sheets from scratch by reading books and doing on-the-ground research. "We taught ourselves the industry," says Rich.

One reason high-quality sheets are so expensive, they learned, is that there are a lot of middlemen involved in making them. By creating a business model whereby the Fulops had the sheets made themselves and sold them directly to consumers on the web, they realized they could keep costs down.

Given their own reaction to the $800 sheets, the Fulops knew that the price point they chose would make or break their business. They suspected many consumers who were outfitting their first home would be willing to pay more than rock-bottom prices for a luxury product that offered more bang for the buck—but they didn't know what the ideal price would be. "When we first got the idea, we were those young shoppers—mid-twenties, just married, newly cohabiting and building our little home," says Vicki. "Rich was in business school, and I was the only one working, so we could definitely not afford those $800 sheets we loved, but we still wanted nice ones! We felt there were others like us, and when we figured out we could bring what we wanted to market—high-quality sheets at an affordable price—we had a feeling we were really onto something."

Instead of guessing what their pricing should be, they went straight to their target customers—a method of market research that cost them nothing but their time. They surveyed five hundred people who were shopping at big-box stores to find out what they were willing to pay for a high-quality set of sheets. They created a simple questionnaire asking about people's sheet-buying habits, then went to the stores they knew people were going to for sheets—such as ABC Carpet & Home, Bed Bath & Beyond, and Crate & Barrel—to survey consumers, and even visited coffee shops, interviewing strangers to round out their sample. To reach online consumers, they created a similar survey on the free tool SurveyMonkey, which they shared on their Facebook pages and asked friends and family to share, as well.

"Our initial model was, we were going to sell the core sheet set for one hundred and ninety-five dollars," says Rich. "What we heard over and over was 'I've got to think about it for two hundred. If you start them at a hundred dollars, then I'll follow the wisdom of crowds.'" Today, the Fulops' Classic Core Set, with a flat sheet, fitted sheet, and two pillowcases in a percale weave, starts at $99 (twin size), and premium products are priced higher.

Fortunately, the internet has made it possible to evaluate whether people will buy your offering without investing in pricey market research. Beyond test marketing products on your own site or on a giant retail marketplace, crowdfunding sites, such as Kickstarter and Indiegogo—where supporters can help you fund a startup by placing preorders for your product—can be an ideal way to put your idea to the test. Just as crowdfunding sites have become well established, so have the businesses they have spawned. In fact, a 2016 Wharton study[6] found that Kickstarter projects had led to the creation of nearly five thousand new for-profit and not-for-profit companies since the site started in 2009, and those companies have generated a collective revenue of $3.4 billion, outside of whatever they raised through crowdfunding.

Crowdfunding proved to be a tremendous resource for the Fulops, who started their business three years ago with $25,000, from their own savings and investments from family. When they realized they needed more money to keep growing the company, they launched a Kickstarter campaign, raising $236,888 in presales of their sheets and giving them strong validation of their idea— proof that their target customers would spend more than $30 for bargain-priced sheets. "It was really just word of mouth," says Vicki. "We had no following."

The Kickstarter campaign validated the unconventional approach to design that distinguished Brooklinen from some of its competitors. Most buyers of linens are women, so many companies' designs are aimed at a female audience. "People don't really try to sell sheets to men," says Rich. But the Fulops realized that style-conscious men do care about sheets—and that the audience is relatively untapped. To attract both men and women as customers, they opted for designs such as stripes and windowpane check patterns that would appeal to both. Today, half of their customers are men. Many buyers are new college grads getting set up in their first apartments and new couples who have added the sheets to their wedding registries.

---

6 Mollick, Ethan R., "Containing Multitudes: The Many Impacts of Kickstarter Funding" (July 11, 2016). Available online at SSRN: ssrn.com/abstract=2808000

As the business grew, the couple moved it from their apartment into a local outlet of WeWork, a coworking hub for freelancers. Creating a small batch of sheets to spread the word to media in New York City, they used Uber to deliver them. As orders poured in, they enlisted freelancers from TaskRabbit to help pack them and delivered them using Zipcar, the car-sharing service. When they needed to make deliveries directly from their office, they used UberRUSH, the ride-sharing service's messenger service. "We've leaned on the sharing economy any way we can," says Rich.

When the work at hand exceeded their ability to keep up, they brought on more freelancers or outsourced. To manage their paid advertising on Facebook, they hired a contractor with specialized expertise. To fill orders, they eventually came to rely on Ruby Has Fulfillment in Long Island City, New York.

Brooklinen's heavy reliance on freelancers and outsourced services allowed it to keep overhead ultra-low as it market-tested its designs and to create a healthy business from the start. "We've been profitable on every sale we made since day one," says Rich. "We put the money back in and have grown and grown." A little over a year after their Kickstarter campaign, when the couple made their first hire, the business hit $750,000 in revenue. By the end of that calendar year, their revenue had reached $2.25 million. The next year, Brooklinen brought in $20 million in revenue. The e-commerce company, which has expanded to products such as duvet covers and down pillows, is no longer staffed entirely by the couple—they have expanded the company to thirty-two people, including a sixteen-person outsourced customer service team in the United States that has received a high level of training in how the couple wants the brand to interact with shoppers—but, says Rich, "we have taken a very strategic approach to keep things lean."

That has allowed the founders to stay close to their customers, who have played a big role in spreading the word on social media and attracting other buyers quickly. "We're trying to keep up with demand," says Rich. Meanwhile, they are launching a second line of premium sheets and are planning some limited edition sets in collaboration with artists.

When I initially spoke with the Fulops, they had not raised venture capital, preferring to stick with their lean freelance model. They felt it helped them stay true to their vision. "We don't have pressure to build out our team to be a certain number or spend money just to spend it," Vicki told me. "We can be really thoughtful and creative and have an end-to-end controlled experience." But as businesses grow and evolve, so does the thinking of the entrepreneurs who start them. As demand for their sheets skyrocketed, the Fulops decided to look for outside capital that would help them keep pace. As word of mouth spread, he says, "it exploded to where we had to hire people. By necessity, things had to change."

The turning point came after a mentor—Frank Rimalovski, executive director of the NYU Entrepreneurial Institute—invested $100,000 in late 2015 on behalf of NYU, Rich's alma mater. Rimalovski introduced Brooklinen to the venture firm FirstMark Capital, which is also an investor in Pinterest and Shopify. After Brooklinen rang up healthy holiday sales in December of its sixth year, the deal closed quickly. By the following March, Brooklinen had raised $10 million in Series A funding from FirstMark Capital.

One thing that helped Brooklinen raise the money was its founders' intimate knowledge of their market. When I reached out to FirstMark Capital founder and managing director Amish Jani to find why he decided to bet on them, he emailed me back the same day.

"Brooklinen is part of the re-invention of retail, where brands form meaningful relationships with their consumers and build a deep sense of community," he wrote. "We were blown away by how they have scaled so efficiently while building a product [that is] truly loved."

Given how far their business has come, the Fulops believe they have built Brooklinen to the point that bringing in an outside investor won't change the character of the brand. "Our investor really gets it, having seen the brand grow and being exposed to it organically," says Vicki. "We found the right person through waiting."

Katherine Krug, thirty-five, also used Kickstarter to market test her idea after she developed debilitating sciatica while working at a startup in San Francisco that kept her deskbound. To alleviate the pain, she conceived a strap to provide back support, using milk jugs and other household materials. She soon realized she was onto a potential startup idea of her own.

When she mentioned her tinkering to friends and acquaintances, Krug discovered that many suffered from back problems and were interested in trying the strap. She hired an industrial designer, whom she met through friends of friends, to create a prototype and then took to Kickstarter to raise funds for her idea.

People were more receptive than she predicted. More than sixteen thousand responded by making pledges or placing preorders. All told, they contributed $1.2 million to her funding campaign. That gave her confidence that the world wanted her product. She also heard from dozens of people who wanted to be distributors and partners, which gave her further proof of concept.

Raising money on Kickstarter enabled Krug to hire a flexible team of contractors to help her bring her ideas to life. The contractors include a marketing firm in Brazil and a virtual assistant in the Philippines. "There's always more to get done," says Krug. "I think a lot of people abandon their vision because they feel so paralyzed by how much there is to do. They get stuck." Fortunately, Krug doesn't have to do it all alone, because she has a great team in place.

If running a crowdfunding campaign isn't ideal for your business, there are other ways to test your idea and leave you with money in reserve if you need to make adjustments.

Justin Goff, thirty-three, did just that when he cofounded an ebook business at a tough point in his life. At the time, a contract gig where he had been doing search engine optimization for a website dried up—and 90% of his income vaporized with it. Meanwhile, he and his girlfriend broke up. At age twenty-seven, he was running out of money and contemplating moving back in with his parents.

But the pressure sparked his creativity, and he soon partnered with his personal trainer to create an ebook called the *31 Day Fat Loss Cure*. His trainer had been in the army and, after taking a desk job, wanted to get back into military shape. The trainer used the short workout he had done in the military to get ripped, and he began sharing his exercise and diet tips with clients like Goff. The duo soon realized they had enough material for a sixty-page ebook and put it up for sale on ClickBank.

With only about $2,000 to invest, Goff had no room for error. He began spending about $100 a day doing Facebook marketing for the book. Through experimentation and careful analysis, he learned to write ads that would attract buyers.

Goff gradually went from burning through $100 a day to losing $50, then $10, and finally breaking even. When an ad finally began making money, he would increase the number of people in his target demographic—college-educated people in their forties and fifties—to whom it was displayed. Soon it was not unusual to make $2,000 a day, he says. Within twelve months, the book was bringing in more than $1 million a year, he says. "Once you learn Facebook ads, it's a great skill to have," says Goff. "You can scale really quickly."

Thinking like Goff and the other entrepreneurs in this chapter is critical if you want to create a million-dollar business, but thinking alone won't get you there. Let's dive into the practicalities of how you can get started.

4

MAKE IT HAPPEN

Born and raised in Texas, Paul Hedrick, twenty-nine, always loved cowboy boots—and his enthusiasm never flagged when he moved to New York City. "If anything, I became more attached to cowboy boots," says Hedrick. "I started wearing them more in office settings to make sure people knew I was the Texan in the office."

Eager to make the most of his degree in math and economics, he took a series of prestigious jobs at companies such as McKinsey & Company and the private equity firm L Catterton, but he still dreamed of starting his own business someday.

At L Catterton, Hedrick did consulting for consumer product companies and found he was drawn to those types of firms. That was when he began thinking about going into the boot business. The cowboy boots he wore were the most expensive item in his wardrobe, and he believed he was forced to pay high prices to buy a decent pair. "There was no one in the category offering a high-quality product at a lower price point," he says. "I realized I should be the one to do it."

In 2014, Hedrick quit his job in New York and began laying the groundwork for what became Tecovas, a business where he sells cowboy boots directly to consumers through an e-commerce website and showroom and at venues, such as concerts. Hedrick, who has a ready smile and genuinely enthusiastic way of telling his story, found that he was good at sales. His business, now based in Austin, Texas, brought in $1 million in annual sales its first year. Because he uses a direct-to-consumer model and does not have to pay middlemen, he can sell the boots for $195 to $235 — substantially less than boots of comparable quality — making them affordable for a wide group of customers. He has also recently introduced higher-end boots, made from materials such as ostrich skin, priced up to $355, as well as a line of belts. The business hit more than $2 million in gross revenue in 2016.

Hedrick is similar to many million-dollar entrepreneurs in that he wasn't sure what he really wanted to do for a living at first. His success lay in listening to his gut instinct, which told him that his passion lay outside of a traditional career, and he was willing to take some chances.

"I was doing cool things at work, and I was making a lot of money," he says. "I liked my job. But I was also willing to leave that job, which I think most people aren't. That is one of the biggest differentiators. Until I had my fingers in the dirt and was creating things, I knew I wasn't going to be fulfilled. That was a big part of my journey."

By taking a few key steps, Hedrick made the successful transition from a traditional career to an entrepreneurial one without throwing his life into upheaval. Many million-dollar entrepreneurs have followed a similar pattern. Here are some of their strategies.

HOW TO FUND THE BUSINESS

Some of the entrepreneurs you've met in this book hit $1 million in revenue in one year or less, working with a CrossFit-like intensity. Others applied the sustained commitment of a yoga practice to get to $1 million. Regardless, most of them realized that initially they would need to pay their bills in another way than with the business and planned accordingly.

If you want to emulate their success, follow their lead. You'll have a lot more creative energy to devote to your business if you are not scrounging to meet expenses in the short term. Having some cash on hand will also allow you to invest in your startup when opportunities present themselves and keep you from pulling the plug on your idea prematurely.

Growing a business can require constant investments at first, and it can take a while before yours can support you. Gallup research[7] shows that only 38% of entrepreneurs rely solely on the income from a startup in its first year, and 54% say another job is their primary way to earn a living. It is only when businesses are two to five years old that most owners rely on them for their primary income. Even then, only 51% get their primary income from the business, and 44% still rely on another job.

So how do you create the financial cushion you need? For people who don't have many business connections and are not experienced in raising money, there are usually four routes.

---

7 Ryan, Ben. "Many US Microbusinesses Depend on Second Job." Gallup.com. April 3, 2014. Available online at: gallup.com/poll/168215/microbusiness-owners-depend-second-job.aspx

ROUTE #1: THE SIDE HUSTLE

Many entrepreneurs start businesses while working full-time for someone else and use their paychecks or a spouse's as funding. "I think it's dangerous to come up with an idea and walk away from a well-paying job if there is no obvious indication this will do well," says Kelly Lester. The flame-haired mother of three and part-time professional actress is also the creator-owner of EasyLunchboxes, an online retail business that she runs from her home in Los Angeles. After eight years, it generates more than $1 million in annual revenue. "I know a lot of people put their heart and soul and all of their money and all of their parents' money into a business that never should have been started in the first place."

Lester, for her part, had sold an earlier internet store that offered decorative switch plates and soaps, in 2006. She dreamed up EasyLunchboxes three years later, when the money from selling that business ran out, the recession hit, and her family needed more income. She used money from her actor husband's paychecks to fund EasyLunchboxes, but, she acknowledges, "We took a big risk."

As her business grew, Lester funded its growth through cash flow. "The orders that continually come in have paid for what we have to order," she says. Although she now has a line of credit with a bank, she hasn't had to dip into it so far, even to fill a recent giant order from Target. That has reduced the financial risks the couple faces. If the lunchboxes don't sell as well as planned through Target, she says, "We'll sell them at cost and walk away." Meanwhile, she'll still have her internet sales to rely on.

UNLOCK THE TIME YOU
NEED TO GET STARTED

If you can't quit your job to start a business, you can still find the time to launch it if you get creative. Consider this: if you set aside just one hour every week to work on your business, at the end of the year you will have devoted fifty-two hours to getting it off the ground—more than enough time to get a preliminary version launched in many cases.

Not disciplined enough to set aside the time every week? Consider devoting an intense chunk of time to getting it all done at once. Techstars, a successful business accelerator, offers a program called Startup Weekend in multiple cities, where you can launch a business over the course of fifty-four hours.

Running a million-dollar one-person business isn't about toiling for long hours. **Unlike in a traditional job, where your pay may be closely tied to the hours you put in, your own business income stems from how smart and selective you are about how you use your time.** Ask Dalton Dale, an entrepreneur who creates interactive attractions like The Uninvited: Awakening, an ultra-scary haunted house set in the basement-level stables of a historic house in Harlem, New York. Dale grew up in a family that put on the best haunted house in the county every Halloween and enjoyed it so much he was inspired to turn the idea into his million-dollar business.

Dale creates his attractions by working in short, intense spurts during key periods, such as May through Halloween, and then taking it a lot easier the rest of the year. When we met, shortly before he launched The Uninvited with a collaborator, Dale, then twenty-six, had been working eighteen hours a day in the month leading up to opening day. During my tour, he charged around like a dervish through sets like the "Secretary Room," where participants get locked in a tiny space with an actress who appears to blow her brains out with a revolver, splattering the ceiling with the gore. "Our normal production period is around nine months," says Dale. "I start my work in January; things pick up in March and get crazy from May onward." But when a launch is not imminent, Dale spends his time planning and creating new attractions with a team of contractors at a far more leisurely pace.

Pacing himself so he can nail the details of each production pays off for Dale. "We were able to double our money!" he told me in an email later.

Meanwhile, he was simultaneously running eight other immersive theater experiences in New York City and other areas at his one-man business, Big Dreamer Productions, which relies on a small army of contractors.

And when we last corresponded, he was working on a brand-new production overseas — The Uninvited: The Delirium Device, a year-round experience in London's West End. He was already trying to raise

£2.25 MM ($2.8 million). "Year-round shows are much more expensive," he noted. But it's well worth the investment to do what he loves. "The days are only going to get longer, but I'm so excited to introduce this unique experience and knock the socks off London's immersive theater scene," he wrote.

TIME-SAVER

Like all million-dollar entrepreneurs, Laszlo Nadler of Tools4Wisdom loves productivity-boosting hacks that let him work less and earn more. This one, designed to prevent email overload, is his automated time-saver of the year. "It will let you permanently de-spam Gmail and Outlook with one broad stroke," he says. The idea is to auto-archive involuntary subscription emails and manually look for what you want, such as discount deals, within the archive folder when needed.

The basic steps in Gmail:

1 Within Gmail settings, go to the search box and click the down arrow. Click the "Filters" tab. Enter your search criteria.

2 Choose "Create a new filter" and in the "Matches" row, enter keyword "unsubscribe."

3 Click "continue" and select "Skip the Inbox (Archive It)."

4 Optional: Select "Also apply filter to matching conversations" (to unclutter *all* past emails).

The basic steps in Outlook:

1 Create a folder with a name like "Low-priority stuff."

2 Right-click any message and click "Rules>Create Rule."

3 Choose a name for the rule and type it in as prompted.

4 Select the conditions as prompted.

5 Select the action as prompted.

6 Save the rule.

The outcome on both mailboxes: 70% reduction of "noise" that disrupts daily focus.

ROUTE #2: KEEP YOUR DAY JOB, LIVE LEAN, AND SAVE

Some entrepreneurs live very frugally and save their money until they can afford to quit and start a business. Paul Hedrick, who is single, didn't have an expensive lifestyle, so he was able to tuck away 20% to 30% of his after-tax earnings while working in his private-equity job. That let him save enough to live on for more than a year—and to make a six-figure investment in his startup.

Giving this level of attention to the financial side of a business is not uncommon among high-revenue solo entrepreneurs. "In terms of attitude and motivations, they treat their businesses like a real business," says Steve King, a partner in Emergent Research, a firm in Walnut Creek, California, that studies the independent workforce. "They have plans, targets, budgets. We see this even in the creative fields. You have to take your business seriously if you are an independent worker or small-business owner."

One reason having cash on hand is so important is that it often takes longer than you think to turn an idea into a money-making business. Hedrick, for instance, ended up doing months of research about what type of boots to offer and how to make them. A key part of this was finding the right boot-making partner. His search took him to León, Mexico, where many major brands make their cowboy boots. There he discovered a group of artisans who ran a factory and teamed up with them. He ended up spending about a week out of every month in León for the first year, working on product development.

Given that he planned to sell only two styles for men and two for women, Hedrick decided to opt for a classic design, avoiding trendy styles that would appeal for only one season. But learning design, even with the help of the artisans, and getting his styles right was not easy. "It took me about sixteen months of full-time work before I launched the brand," recalls Hedrick. "It took more than two times longer than I thought, but I have no regrets."

Hedrick stretched the cash in his bank account, keeping his promotion costs down by focusing on building a mailing list. He put up a website about six months before launch and asked friends and family to visit it, share their email addresses, and spread the word. He incentivized people to sign up by giving friends and family $10 in "Tecovas credit" every time they got someone new to join the list. "It was a lean, costless way to encourage a lot of people to join," he says. Where he invested his money, he says, was in creating the right image for the brand through design and photography. "The big differentiator for us as a brand was showing people the boots really are high end." And offering the credits for referrals paid off. Hedrick estimates that Tecovas hit six-figure sales in the first few months.

After Tecovas made its first $100,000 in sales, Hedrick brought in an equity partner—Branden Windle, a friend who worked for an angel investor. His partner's focus on growth and marketing has helped Hedrick accelerate the company's progress. He says, "My philosophy was, we needed to prove we can get real traction."

Sure, it was easier for Hedrick to save and raise money than it is for many, given his high-paying day job. But you can save seed money even if you're not in a finance career. Allen Walton, the founder of SpyGuy, managed to sock away the money he used to start his security camera store while working in a similar shop by simply living lean and choosing to start a business that does not require much startup capital.

WHAT IF YOU HAVE FAMILY AND
HEALTH CARE TO COVER?

If you have dependents to support, it will be more difficult to free up the money needed to launch a business. I know—as I've mentioned, I've got four children myself—and buying groceries and soccer cleats can really add up. That doesn't mean it's impossible. Some entrepreneurs tap retirement funds, rely on a spouse's income, or use severance pay to invest in a business while juggling the financial responsibilities that come with having children.

As someone who has been self-employed for about ten years and purchased health insurance for a family of six during most of that time, either through a broker or directly through an insurance company, I know the pain that the United States' health-care crisis can inflict. At one point, my family was paying more than $3,100 a month for our premium until we finally switched to a high-deductible plan and tax-advantaged health savings account to cover out-of-pocket costs. Even then, our premium was close to $2,000 a month.

I'm well aware that many families can't afford the kind of premiums we paid, and the costs may be prohibitive if you're running a startup. Before my husband went in-house and obtained our health insurance through his job, it was a stretch for us, too. The only way we could make those premiums was to live well below our means. Opening the envelope with our annual premium increase literally made me gasp every year. One year, the increase was $600 per month!

Some US entrepreneurs may benefit from subsidies under the Affordable Care Act, but if your family income puts them out of reach, or you live in a very high-cost state, you will have to get creative. The following strategies won't fill the giant gaps in the health-care system or solve the challenges of coping with a serious illness or condition, but they have helped my family take a small measure of control over our health-care situation.

MAKE FITNESS PART OF YOUR ROUTINE

Finding some fitness activities you will stick with, whatever they are, is a good practice to support your health. One of the best investments in our budget was joining a local YMCA about five minutes from our home with many offerings that appeal to us, from "family boot camp" to my daughter's gymnastics team. It costs about $100 a month. It's not a fancy place, but we all use it constantly because it is so convenient.

INVEST IN A HEALTHY DIET

Many of the major health problems people face in industrialized countries are tied to diet in some way and typically linked to eating a diet heavy in processed foods and sugar. To do what we can to avoid them, we try to eat fresh, unprocessed foods most of the time.

By joining Costco, we can afford many organic foods even with a family of six. (Previously, we belonged to an organic food co-op, another economical alternative.) Although my husband and I used to be frequent restaurant-goers, we've increasingly found we prefer cooking at home, in part because there are fewer unhealthy ingredients added to our food. On the occasions when we want to go out to eat, we opt for restaurants that serve high-quality, fresh food—depending on the cuisine, you can find them across the price spectrum.

FIND LOW-COST STRESS-REDUCTION STRATEGIES

Running a business—even a very successful one—comes with many pressures, and it's easy to let stress creep up on you. Over time, that stress can erode your health. I have found that getting occasional massages at a student clinic ($35) is a low-cost way to decompress. Going to yoga classes at my YMCA also proved to be a great stress reliever, once I got past my initial fear that they would be too "slow" and boring. I found that Vinyasa or flow yoga was fast-paced enough to keep me engaged.

BUILD AN ALTERNATIVE HEALTH TEAM

In some medical groups, I have noticed doctors are under heavy pressure to overprescribe to keep patients in "compliance" with accepted treatment plans. When I have had doubts about whether a drug is necessary, I have on occasion turned to a very experienced independent functional medicine physician, who accepts cash payments only, for a second opinion. This isn't inexpensive, but I trust what he says. Given the high cost of prescription drugs, and the unwanted side effects some may cause, I believe that getting his advice has helped us keep costs in check without compromising anyone's health and has more than paid for itself. Many people find it unaffordable to see a physician who does not accept insurance, so if this option is not available to you, try looking for a doctor you trust within your insurance network. It took me two years of searching, but I recently found an osteopath in private practice who accepts our insurance, which has brought down the cost of getting second opinions.

GET ROUTINE SCREENINGS AND PLAN FOR NONEMERGENT MEDICAL EXPENSES

You can't prevent every problem through screening, but it is always better to catch health issues early—before they become more serious and more expensive to treat.

One criticism of high-deductible plans is that people do not get needed care because they can't afford the deductibles. Timing major medical expenses can help you make the most of your plan. For instance, I recently had to take a medical test that costs about $2,000 out of pocket, which we will cover with money we put in our HSA. Knowing that this amount was applied to our deductible, I grouped other medical visits and tests for family members around it on the calendar, so we hit the deductible early in the year. To do this, I postponed nonurgent appointments that physicians had suggested the prior year. Because we tackled many of these appointments this year, I am hoping that next year we will have a light year in terms of medical costs and not get anywhere near our deductible. I would not recommend this approach if you have a time-sensitive medical problem, but it can help you stretch your health-care budget for non-urgent appointments and tests.

Jonathan Johnson, fifty-seven, a former corporate salesman and father of two from Chico, California, took the first steps toward creating two related e-commerce businesses that together now generate $2.8 million in revenue while he was still working in real estate finance. He launched the businesses not long before the global economic collapse, when he began to fear his industry was getting shaky and saw he might need another source of income.

To come up with an e-commerce idea, he looked back at what he had done before. Prior to working in real estate, Johnson had a job in medical sales, and he decided to repurpose that experience in selling medical supplies to prisons, as well as some law enforcement supplies. This time around, he opted to sell gear to protect hospital employees from contact with potentially infectious blood and other medical supplies, as well as supplies for law enforcement, such as riot helmets. While still employed, he registered his business, DirectGov Source, with the state and added himself to a list of government vendors of medical equipment.

"Sure enough, about two weeks later I get an order from the franchise tax board," recalls Johnson. "They wanted to order some defibrillators. They knew what they wanted—the model number, the part number, how many they needed." Johnson quickly obtained a new business Visa account and hurried to buy the devices. "That started the ball rolling," he says.

Eager to find a new source of income while he was still employed, Johnson made a hundred cold calls a day to introduce himself to police departments around the country. By that time, all of the employees who reported to him had either resigned or been let go, and he had little work to do as a branch manager for his company. When he got the call from a regional manager that his branch was being closed, he was prepared. "I was set up at the house," he says. "I had a ten-month lead. I was good to go at that point."

The first year, Johnson's family relied mainly on savings and income from his wife's work. His business brought in only $30,000 in gross sales and $8,000 in income, he recalls. The couple had two sons, then teens, to support. "It was scary," he says, but he felt he had no other option.

His wife, Dyana, who'd always supported the idea of his launching the startup, asked at one point if the business was going to work. "I was having some doubts," Johnson admits. "Then I happened to land this contract with the California Highway Patrol. That gave me some confidence." Each time he sold a new product, he would try to determine if there was interest from other police departments. Often, he noticed, they took a follow-the-leader approach, and if one department started using something, others would adopt it, too. "From there on, things started to grow," he recalls.

To stay focused, Johnson wrote a business plan, which he still tries to follow. About two years after launching his first site, he opened a second one, PPEKits.com, which focuses solely on protective gear. Noticing that many government clients wanted customized infection-prevention kits, he offered them the option of customizing their own to stand out. His younger son helped him put together kits in the garage at night, but when demand increased he turned to a service that employed adults with disabilities to do the assembly. As the business continued to expand, Johnson needed help with processing orders and bookkeeping, so he brought in an assistant from a temp agency. Instead of working from home, he moved into a 1,500-square-foot office and warehouse.

"One thing I realized is, you can't stop growth," he says. "It's an amazing thing once it happens. You have to prepare yourself."

Johnson didn't have much startup capital, so he built the businesses in a way that didn't require him to buy much inventory. He relies mostly on a drop shipper to process orders. "My business is probably 90% drop shipped," says Johnson. That means if he gets a purchase order for five hundred items from a government agency, he submits the order to a manufacturer who will send the goods straight to the client. He'll then pay the manufacturer and collect the money owed by the government. "The government may pay you late, but you always get paid," says Johnson.

Three years after starting the business, he was able to obtain a line of credit with a bank, which helps him with cash flow if payments arrive slowly. The initial line was only $25,000, but he stuck with the same bank as his business grew, and his lender eventually extended that to $250,000. Having government clients worked in his favor. "That was one thing the bank liked—the stability of the client base," says Johnson.

Johnson has found the line of credit is a nice safety net, in case there is a delay in getting paid by clients and he needs to pay suppliers. Still, he is cautious about tapping it, because he doesn't like the pressure of owing someone else money.

"I used the line of credit only in situations where we absolutely had to," he says. "I don't use it to meet payroll or for frivolous things. I don't use it to stock inventory." He does use it to keep his vendors paid on time. As he well knows, keeping those relationships strong goes a long way toward enabling him to keep his clients happy.

As technology gets cheaper, the cost of starting a business keeps declining, so you may need less financing than you think. If you have done your homework and are serious about your business, putting money into your startup may be the smartest investment you ever make.

FOCUS ON THE GOAL

Like Johnson, Laszlo Nadler started a lucrative business while working full-time and raising a family. How did he pull it off? He squeezed the work in on weekends and managed to spend less time at the office over a couple of years. The key? **Constantly identifying ways to avoid unimportant activities, like manually doing unnecessary email and A/B testing (which compares two versions of a web page to see which one consumers like best).** (See chapter 5 [page 146] for more on A/B testing.) He knew that his doubling up was only temporary and saw it as an investment in his long-term liberation from the daily grind.

If you are doubling up, as he did, you too can lighten your load by taking inventory of time wasters that eat up time you could spend on the business—and rooting them out. Are you spending a lot of time scheduling appointments? Consider using a low-cost scheduling app like ScheduleOnce, which allows business contacts to view your public schedule and select a time that works for them. Are you wasting a lot of time making international calls on free phone services that never seem to work and disconnect you? Try switching to Globafy, a free service that lets you set up conference bridges that are local to both you and the countries of the other people meeting on the line. Are you wasting time following up with prospects to see if they read your email? Try a free service like

Streak for Gmail, which tells you whether they actually opened it and also lets you stay on top of processes like follow-up that you might otherwise lose track of. For every tedious task you're doing, there probably is an app that can help you eliminate it or reduce the time it takes, if you're willing to do some digging. There's even an app called Williams&Harricks that you can use to send demand letters to clients who have failed to pay you for work and haven't responded to a gentler approach.

Managing the research projects that come with running a business, such as finding helpful apps, may sound overwhelming, but there are ways to make it fun for yourself. "You can turn a boring, dry topic into an exciting one if you can change your question to: What creative ideas will help improve my quality of life?" Nadler says.

It may take some commitment to liberate time to recharge. To keep his fast-growing business from devouring his free time, Nadler relies on virtual assistants and uses automation. "I automated my customer emails so I can reach out to every customer with a very personal letter, giving them a chance to reply directly to me," he explains. That enables Nadler to build and control his mailing list. Otherwise, the online marketplace through which he sells his planners effectively controls the consumer relationship.

ROUTE #3: GET OTHERS TO INVEST

Sometimes, starting a business may require more money than you can reasonably come up with on your own, no matter how many nights you dine on mac and cheese. In that case, you will need to find outside backers. When Paul Hedrick exhausted his own funds, for instance, he found that his expertise in running an ultra-lean, high-profit business made it very attractive to outside backers. He turned to private investors, known as angels, whom he knew through his business dealings, and sold them a small stake in his business in exchange for cash, then raised $1.2 million more in another round later, bringing the total to more than $1.8 million in equity funding. The funding has allowed him to add staff. A full year after his launch, he realized it was too difficult to handle business in Mexico by himself and hired a production manager who is based there. He has also hired someone to help him with finance, and three customer service team members—which is a good thing given that revenue is growing exponentially.

Dalton Dale, the haunted house impresario—who had done stage work for Broadway shows—cold-called connections in the theater business to raise the $1 million he needed to create his premium haunted house experience. "I only had one month to raise $1 million," he says. But pressure spurred him on and encouraged him to invest in taking the steps necessary to attract investors. It cost $25,000 in legal fees to create the offering documents alone.

There are many excellent books on how to attract and work with investors, such as attorney Andrew Sherman's *Raising Capital* (Amacom, 2012). If you don't have many business connections in the finance world or you lack the nerve to call strangers and persuade them to invest in your idea, borrowing money from your friends and family or selling them a piece of your business is generally the most accessible option. Just make sure you don't end up destroying personal relationships by borrowing money you can't pay back. Also get legal advice on how best to structure an equity deal from an attorney who is well versed in these transactions, so you don't sell too much of the business and end up losing control.

ROUTE #4: EXPLORE OTHER FINANCING OPTIONS

Selling equity is just one way to raise money. If your business idea is very innovative, one great way to rustle up cash is by entering business plan competitions that offer prize money. Local competitions take place in many areas and are often connected with universities in the area. Sites such as BizPlanCompetitions (bizplancompetitions.com) can help you find contests you may qualify for. I know a number of entrepreneurs who make it a regular habit to enter such competitions. Those with great business plans often rack up multiple wins—and prize money that doesn't have to be paid back. (You *will* have to pay taxes on it, so make sure you get advice from your accountant on how much to set aside.) Some of the prizes can be quite substantial and even into the six-figure range. In some cases, winners may have to provide the sponsors with equity, so make sure you know what you would be giving up before you enter.

It is very difficult to get a bank to loan you money when you don't have much of a business established, so that is not usually a realistic option for a brand-new startup. If you have good credit and access to credit cards, however, it is possible to borrow the funding you need that way. Many founders of startups do this. Those who have excellent credit can often get deals with 0% interest for a limited period, keeping the cost of borrowing to the absolute minimum.

If you go this route, do so cautiously and never borrow more than you can reasonably pay back. Many people don't know that even if you use a small-business credit card, you very likely signed a card holder's agreement in which the fine print holds you personally responsible for the debts on the card. It is next to impossible to get a small-business card that does not require a personal guarantee. That means that even if the business goes under, you will need to pay the balance on your card—which could be quite difficult if you've just lost your income source.

For several years I have written a Q&A column on a website for credit card users where I answer letters from readers. Some of the most tragic questions I receive are from readers who have maxed out their cards for a business that failed several years ago and are now struggling to make the payments or have stopped making them and are being pursued by the lenders. Bankruptcy laws have gotten tougher in recent years, and it is difficult to get out of paying, no matter how dire your circumstances, so it's not worth putting yourself at risk of being in heavy debt for years.

You're better off growing your business more slowly and funding growth out of cash flow. Despite the popular image of entrepreneurs being high rollers, many million-dollar entrepreneurs are conservative about borrowing, doing it only when absolutely imperative. "I'm very anti-debt," says Matt Friel, one of the million-dollar e-commerce entrepreneurs you'll meet later. "I tend to pay everything up front. If I buy inventory, I pay cash for it." Operating this way has its benefits. He has noticed that his suppliers come to him first with great inventory because he pays so quickly.

Crowdfunding is another option worth exploring. For many entrepreneurs, preselling a product on a site like Kickstarter or Indiegogo is a good way to generate the money they need to actually produce it. Typically, donation-based sites require entrepreneurs to consider the contributions made as pledges, with the products shipped as gifts that go to people who provide set levels of support—almost like the canvas tote bags you can opt to receive if you support your favorite museum.

Though it might seem optional to send a gift offered in return for a pledge, in reality the consumers who make pledges expect to get the products in a timely manner, as if they had ordered it from an e-commerce merchant. If you're a first-time entrepreneur, you may hit unexpected bumps in producing your product and not be able to meet these expectations—which may frustrate your fan base. So if you want to raise money on a donation-based crowdfunding site, it is important to put a good communication strategy in place to keep donors informed about your progress. That means posting progress reports on the site and strategic email messaging. Otherwise, you could find yourself spending all of your time managing complaints that damage the brand you are trying to build.

The other type of crowdfunding involves selling equity to investors. Equity crowdfunding sites can save you the work of finding private investors if you don't have a lot of connections. However, if you sell equity, you need to get good advice from a lawyer experienced in these transactions. Many entrepreneurs, unable to project what their business could be worth in the future, sell too much equity for too little money when they are starting out and hungry for cash. If your business takes off, you will regret this. Another caution: there are many entrepreneurs who have an inflated sense of what their business is worth. They can kill deals with equity investors by making unreasonable demands. A smart advisor will help you look out for your best interests while securing the funding you need.

EXPERIMENT AND REVISE

One reason you will need multiple sources of cash during the launch phase is that not everything you try in your business will work the first time. **You may have to experiment and revise a few times to create a salable product and develop a viable business.** Many entrepreneurs in product-based businesses find they have to keep tweaking their product to get it right before it finally takes off. You need to bake time into the process to allow for multiple versions, and some money to pay for your experiments. There might not just be a version 2.0. There could be a version 99.0.

Ask Matt LaCasse, thirty. When he woke up in the mood to make pancakes one morning, he came to a realization: "Everything that was 'just add water' was really gross and bad for you," he recalls. LaCasse and his wife, Lizzi Ackerman, twenty-nine, decided to do something about that. The couple, who had met as college students, began experimenting with their own pancake mix. "There is not a lot of innovation in this space," says LaCasse. Excited about creating a better product, they incorporated Birch Benders, a natural and organic brand, six years ago, using a local attorney and tapping their own savings to get started. Although Birch Benders used an attorney to incorporate, you don't necessarily have to do so, given the abundance of sites, such as BizFilings and LegalZoom.com, that will allow you to set up a business entity online. However, get professional advice on the right legal structure for your type of firm from an attorney and an accountant, as the structure you choose will have bearing on your potential liabilities and the amount of taxes you pay.

Sold nationwide in stores such as Whole Foods, Target, and ShopRite, Birch Benders now has annual revenue "well into the seven figures, close to eight," according to LaCasse. Beyond traditional pancake recipes like buttermilk, the duo have come up with vegan, paleo, gluten-free, and high-protein versions. Working with partners such as Target, they have developed flavors such as pumpkin spice. But it took a while to get there.

ASK YOUR TARGET CUSTOMER—AND LISTEN

LaCasse, who'd been a math major, was working at a farm-to-table restaurant when he and Ackerman began working on their mixes; meanwhile, she was studying organic chemistry. Neither had much experience in the food manufacturing business, so they created double-blind taste tests for themselves to make sure they were using the ideal ingredients. "We made sure each ingredient was the absolutely best one on the planet for a given recipe," says Ackerman.

Getting their recipes right took persistence beyond the point at which many people might give up. For the paleo mix, created in collaboration with Whole Foods, "This was our ninety-ninth recipe," recounts Ackerman.

The couple didn't have a lot of resources at their disposal; from the start, they used the kitchen of their rented house as a laboratory, to their landlord's consternation. "Our cover was blown when an eighteen-wheeler pulled into our driveway with pallets," recalls LaCasse. Often, they had to take business calls while a musician roommate, a member of an electronic band, played the saxophone — but they didn't let that impede their progress. "It was a crazy time," recalls Ackerman.

To support the sales of their products, they did demos at their local Whole Foods. "We would wake up and do two to three demos a day," recalls Ackerman. As they did this, they gathered useful consumer feedback on every aspect of their product.

EVOLVE THE PRODUCT PRESENTATION

Through their demos, LaCasse and Ackerman learned that their prices were too high when they initially sold the mix in jars. They transitioned to a resealable pouch and eventually, after some experimenting, hired a branding agency to get it right. When I met them, they were on version 5.0 of the package — one that includes quirky pictures, including characters who tell a colorful story about the brand. Birch Benders, in case you are wondering, is named for something LaCasse liked to do when growing up in Maine: bending supple birch trees as he played with them — a story that's told on the pouches.

PRICE RIGHT FOR PERCEIVED VALUE

The couple experimented with the size of their packages, which, they discovered, didn't sell well at twenty-four ounces. It was only when they shrunk them down to sixteen ounces—which made them more affordable—that sales took off.

They also experimented with pricing. Because the company uses high-end ingredients, it has to charge more than mass-market brands. "The right price point was really important," says LaCasse. The sixteen-ounce packages of the specialty mixes, such as gluten-free, paleo, and high-protein, now retail for about $5.99 at Whole Foods, while the other mixes, such as pumpkin spice and classic, are about $4.99. A new non-GMO but nonorganic twenty-four-ounce package retails for about $3.99 in grocery stores.

At times, all of the couple's experimenting has meant putting other important things on hold—like the honeymoon to Mt. Kilimanjaro they were about to take when I met them. That was a year after they got married—but they viewed that as a small inconvenience. "To see your ideas and dreams come to fruition is a big reward," says LaCasse.

KNOW WHEN TO CONTRACT FOR PRODUCTION, FULFILLMENT, DELIVERY

By using a copacker, a manufacturer that makes and packages the mixes, the couple ran their ultra-lean startup as the only employees until three years after they incorporated, getting very close to seven figures on their own. Like other million-dollar food entrepreneurs, they learned it was more cost-effective to use a copacker than to try to become manufacturers, because they lacked the economies of scale that giant food makers have. Since then, they have grown the business to five employees, and they expect to hire more as they scale up. To pull that off, they are no longer relying only on their own money; they have raised venture capital from Boulder Food Group and other investors in two rounds of funding.

LaCasse and Ackerman never intended to manufacture the product on their own, which would be a giant undertaking. From the get-go, they planned to hire a copacker, says Ackerman. But finding one that would do tiny runs of a thousand packages was challenging. When she cold-called copackers around the country, recalls Ackerman, "Most of them laughed in my face." After working with a local copacker initially, they switched to a larger one in California who really believed in their brand and was patient enough do tiny runs for several years. Later they added another copacker in Chicago, to add redundancy to the business as a safeguard. In the packaged food industry, the standard profit margin—after paying for ingredients, copacking costs, and shipping—is 40%. "We like to get higher than 40% personally—but it takes a lot of research," LaCasse added. One thing that has helped boost the profit margin has been accessing bulk ingredients as the company has scaled.

With their pancake business taking off, the couple is setting their sights on new products. "We have a lot in the works besides pancakes," says Ackerman.

AMPLIFY WHAT WORKS

When you're just starting your business, the first few sales you make may strike you as a sort of miracle, especially if you have never run a business before. But eventually, if you keep making sales, you'll realize that they are not a fluke or beginner's luck.

Chances are you are doing something right. Once you figure out exactly what that something is, amplifying what you're doing will help you scale up your revenue, even without hiring employees. There are many ways to do this.

SOCIAL ADVERTISING

Once Paul Hedrick, the cowboy boot maker, started attracting a steady stream of customers to his Tecovas website, he began investing in paid ads on Facebook and Google to build his store's online presence. Although he handled the paid advertising campaigns himself in the beginning, he eventually hired a consultant with expertise in social media advertising buying for customer acquisition to draw even more visitors to his store. That reduced the risk of paying for ads that were duds and didn't attract many people. "You're better off using an agency or consultant until you can afford [to employ an expert] to do it in-house," Hedrick says.

USE A MAJOR ONLINE RETAILER

Some million-dollar entrepreneurs find that they can amplify their impact by establishing a presence on a major online retail site. That is what Kelly Lester, founder of EasyLunchboxes, did. She started out trying to sell her lunchboxes on her own website and succeeded in attracting customers, but realized that partnering with a bigger site would help her grow the business more quickly. What ultimately helped her was joining the same giant e-tailer's vendor program, which instantly put her in front of millions of customers and, she found, worked out better for her financially than using the site's fulfillment service.

PICK THE RIGHT ONLINE
COMMUNITY PLATFORM(S)

If you want to build a million-dollar, one-person business, social media can be a powerful tool—as long as you use it judiciously. Million-dollar entrepreneurs stay focused and understand which platforms their ideal customers actually use and value most—and devote their time to the ones that deliver the greatest return on their investment of time and money.

This can take some experimenting and strategic thinking. If you run a promotion on Facebook that brings in hordes of customers, for example, but they are almost all bargain hunters who only show up one time to get the discount offered, then you might be better off trying other platforms. If you aim to attract affluent consumers, it could be that your ideal customers mostly hang out on a niche site for aviation aficionados or lovers of fine wines. You will be able to determine that only by testing platforms to see which are the most effective for your business idea. Asking contacts in the field which sites they like may introduce you to some new ones you haven't considered.

Once you have a good understanding of which platforms pay off most for you, concentrate on just one or two. By establishing an active presence and posting frequently, you'll gradually build a strong and consistent presence for your brand—and an active dialogue with customers and prospects.

BUILD RELATIONSHIPS WITH
SOCIAL MEDIA INFLUENCERS

Using social media has helped Lester amplify her message in innumerable ways. When she first started EasyLunchboxes, she often poked around in search engines for mentions of lunch containers and lunch boxes to see which brands had the best internet presence. She discovered that the brands ranked highest in Google often got mentioned in independent blogs. "I learned that if you can get social media mentions and links back to your website, Google recognizes those things," she says. That, in turn, pulls the website higher in search engine results pages, she found.

After seeing how important it was to get mentioned by bloggers, she was determined to attract their attention, too. "I started connecting with bloggers in a one-on-one, extremely friendly, uncorporate way," she says. "I wrote to them like a fellow mom and, if I did indeed love their blog, said stuff like, 'Hey, I love your pictures. Your family is beautiful. I'd like you to feature my lunchboxes. Is this something you can use?' I reached out to them like a person."

That approach worked for her business—and also enriched her life personally. "The majority of bloggers I've worked with are always delighted and amazed that the owner of what they think is a big company—even though it's me in my den—is actually communicating with them," says Lester. "I'm good friends with a number of these original bloggers I contacted. They continue to support EasyLunchboxes and share my products. This has multiplied like a spiderweb."

CREATE VISUAL SOCIAL MEDIA

The world of social media is ever changing — and it's important to keep up. Although many bloggers Lester knows still post regularly on relevant topics, including lunch packing, some have slowed down. "With Instagram and Pinterest, many people are cutting to the chase and only posting pictures and commentary," says Lester.

Making the most of influencers' visual social media has helped Lester spread the word. Avid foodie moms often share pictures on Pinterest and Instagram of the photogenic meals they pack in her lunchboxes — and she, in turn, promotes these images. "I got lucky," she says. "People take pictures of what they are eating." She also reaches out to YouTube video bloggers. Such efforts have helped her become one of the top lunchbox sellers on the giant retail site where she runs her store.

Meghan Telpner has also found video to be a very useful tool for her businesses, MeghanTelpner.com and the Academy of Culinary Nutrition (CulinaryNutrition.com). After getting sick on a trip to Africa, the Toronto resident received a surprising diagnosis: she was suffering from Crohn's disease. Telpner, now thirty-seven, was working in advertising at the time but had to leave her job when her condition left her too sick to work. "I was going to doctors and no one could help me," she recalls. "I was just twenty-six and had to figure it out."

That experience started Telpner on a journey of studying holistic nutrition and learning to manage her illness so effectively that, after making many dietary and lifestyle changes, she is now symptom-free. Nine years ago, she started MeghanTelpner.com, a hub of information on health and wellness, and three years ago, she launched the Academy of Culinary Nutrition, which has also become a seven-figure business. The academy was a solo operation until six years ago, when she hired a full-time assistant to help her scale.

Telpner originally started her business with the idea of creating a community around food, offering cooking classes several days a week from her tiny kitchen. At the time, she was eliminating gluten and dairy from her diet—a challenging task in a world of processed foods with long ingredient lists. She focused on introducing fresh, healthy dishes she was able to enjoy with friends, so people making similar dietary choices didn't have to feel like the odd one out every time they dined with others.

As Telpner expanded the site, she attracted readers with a variety of health concerns. "People are waking up to the fact that as a society we're not feeling well," she says. Passionate about keeping her followers informed, Telpner blogged every day, eventually churning out more than two thousand posts. Telpner, who has a degree in fashion marketing, made the site entertaining, adding photos of herself in colorful vintage clothes; shots of her stylish clinical nutritionist husband; recipes for all-natural, DIY beauty products; and information on the practices, from yoga to infrared saunas, that have kept her from suffering flare-ups. At the same time, she took strong stands on issues that matter to her, from the ingredients in baby lotion to breakfasts that include Nutella.

Looking to reach a bigger audience, Telpner introduced her first online class—on her three-day Green Smoothie Cleanse—the same year she launched the site. About two hundred people signed up, paying $10. *This is incredible*, she said to herself. She recalls, "That was my introduction to 'How do we scale this?'"

Not long after that, Telpner began filming cooking demonstrations in her kitchen and soon started a YouTube channel. "My early videos were so embarrassing," she says. "I was doing them all myself. They were me, alone, in my kitchen." But with practice, she got better and better at making videos. With health enthusiasts from around the world and other fans contacting her for advice, she created a video-based tutorial program. Three years ago, she opened the online Academy of Culinary Nutrition, offering students a certification when they completed the program. The program costs $1,850 to $3,600, depending on whether students sign up for private coaching. As of December 2016, more than 1,100 students had graduated from forty-three countries.

Meanwhile, to spread her message even further, Telpner began writing books. Four years ago, she wrote a book called *UnDiet: Eat Your Way to Vibrant Health*. She wrote another book, *The UnDiet Cookbook*, two years later. Each move she makes contributes to her positive, inspiring message about taking charge of one's own health and wellness.

BUILD A STEADY INCOME

One of the biggest challenges of creating a successful one-person business is getting to the point where you can live on the income the business brings in, so you don't have to hold other jobs as well. That can take some time. But what if you can't wait—because you have no job and need to make a full-time living now to support yourself, and maybe even a family? Living on what you bring in through the business is definitely possible, but you will need to figure out how to get money flowing into your business more quickly.

CONSULT A SMALL-BUSINESS ACCOUNTANT

One important part of building the kind of business that can support you is finding a good accountant, preferably one who works with small businesses frequently. So how do you find one? Ask other business owners for a referral to someone they trust. Ideally, find someone local who can get to know you and your business. Jeffrey Rinz, a broker of industrial equipment whom you'll meet later in the book, recommends finding an accountant who also runs a small business. His own accountant is a CPA who owns two or three companies. "She's got real-life experience to give me," says Rinz.

How will you know you've found a good accountant? "The prospective accountant should ask questions about your business, listen carefully, and be responsive to what they perceive to be your needs," says CPA Paul Gevertzman, a tax partner at Anchin, Block & Anchin, a New York City accounting firm. "You want someone who has taken the time to research your business and has come prepared. If they offer to review your tax and financial papers and present some suggestions, take them up on it, but get a nondisclosure agreement from them first."

After the meeting, Gevertzman advises, ask the accountant follow-up questions and see how quickly he or she responds and if the answers satisfy you. "If they aren't going the extra mile on all these points when they are trying to land you as a client, don't expect to get great service once you are a client," he says. Your ideal accountant will be someone who is very punctual and reminds you of upcoming tax deadlines, instead of needing to be reminded. Someone you need to keep after, no matter how proficient in accounting, will ultimately become more of a problem than a help.

If you succeed in running a high-revenue, one-person business with very lean overhead, it is likely to be profitable — and you will owe taxes on those profits. If your business is so successful you end up in a high tax bracket, without good accounting advice you may not keep much of what you bring in, which can prevent you from reinvesting in your business. A good accountant will help you stay informed about the deductions you should be taking. "You know your business, but there are many things you may not be aware of," says Gevertzman. "If you spend your time trying to research it all yourself, you are taking your time away from growing your business."

As your revenue grows, you'll also need good advice on the ideal business structure to minimize your taxes. Many people start sole proprietorships as LLCs because it's easy to do so. However, as their revenue grows, it sometimes makes sense to transition from paying taxes as an LLC to doing so as an S Corporation. Although there are added record-keeping burdens to maintaining S Corp status, many owners experience significant tax savings. It is best to get advice on this sooner rather than later, especially if your business is growing quickly. "It was the best move I ever made," says Jonathan Johnson, who transitioned to an S Corp three years ago. Although the year he made the changes was challenging because of the paperwork and associated costs, he says, "It really made a difference."

Mastering the financial side of your business may be a bit overwhelming if you are more of a creative, visionary type. The good news is you don't have to tackle all of it at once. When you are just starting out and have only a few customers, the financial side of things is pretty easy. Plus, there are many excellent, inexpensive, cloud-based software programs that can keep your finances organized. And if you really can't face any of it, it is easy to find a bookkeeper or accountant to handle it for you by asking other business owners.

THE POWER OF CASH FLOW

To build a steady income for yourself, you have to establish strong cash flow in your business. If you can't do that, you won't be able to pay your bills or take money out of the business when you need it.

Mastering cash flow can be difficult, given that you may be part of an industry in which you don't get paid right away. "A fairly large percentage of small businesses end up in some sort of crisis over cash in the first couple of years of their existence," says Dave Kurrasch, a former senior vice president at a national bank and president of the consultancy Global Payments Advisors in Scottsdale, Arizona.

Many new owners don't fully understand that revenue and cash flow are not one and the same. In many cases, if you invoice customers for work you've done, you may not get paid for thirty days or more, he notes. In the meantime, you have to pay your bills. "If you desperately need that money to pay your staff or the electricity bill, that thirty-day difference can be very damaging," says Kurrasch.

HOW TO IMPROVE YOUR CASH FLOW

Know where you are likely to stand, and plan ahead.

LOOK AHEAD SIX TO TWELVE MONTHS

Most entrepreneurs tend to be overly optimistic, so learn how to use the forecasting tools in your accounting software to figure out how much cash is really coming into the business and how much you will need to pay for planned costs, such as new equipment purchases and talent you expect to add.

If you don't have the time, ask your accountant to do it for you. It'll be money well spent. "Small-business owners are so busy running their businesses that they are not really thinking about two, three, or four months from now," says Kurrasch. "They are just thinking about getting through today." However, that puts them at a disadvantage when it comes to surviving. "Anybody who starts a business should do some planning," he says. That should include a six- to twelve-month forecast of how much cash you will have flowing through the business. If you're selling T-shirts, that means looking at how many shirts you're likely to sell, what revenue you're likely to produce, and when you will get that money. This will tell you whether you can afford to restock the T-shirts now or if you need to wait a while.

FIND WAYS TO SPEED PAYMENTS

When you're busy, it's easy to let invoicing slide, but that's dangerous for the survival of your business. You will greatly improve your cash flow if you establish a regular discipline of invoicing, collecting payments, and getting them into the bank, says Dave Kurrasch. "If you can invoice a customer frequently and on time, you're better off," he says.

Letting your invoicing slip by even a week because you're busy can put you in a cash crunch. Your client's payment period starts from the date on the invoice.

To get paid more quickly, consider using tools that let you accept credit cards, such as Square or Apple Pay. Scanning checks remotely through mobile payment tools that let you deposit them directly in the bank can also accelerate your cash flow. Some invoicing software programs also allow you to accept credit cards or ACH payments (automatic debits from customers' bank accounts).

Offering options for payment, such as paying by credit card, may inspire customers who are experiencing cash-flow problems to pay you more quickly, Kurrasch says, but you also have to pay attention to how much the processing fees affect your profit margins. The processing fee for many cards is 2.5%. "If you have a 2% margin in your business, being paid by credit card wipes out your margin," notes Kurrasch. "If your business has a 50% margin, it's affordable to take a credit card to get paid." Some accounting software programs, such as FreshBooks and QuickBooks, allow you to manually check a box offering the option to pay by credit cards, so take advantage of it. It allows you the option of offering credit card payments only when necessary.

PAY YOUR BILLS MORE SLOWLY

Using cash for purchases or a debit card drains your bank account immediately. And if you receive bills that give you thirty days to pay, don't send the check the first week. Wait until you're close to the deadline, but not in danger of paying late, except with crucial vendors who may give you priority for paying early. Paying your bills on a low- or zero-interest credit card and even using checks can buy you more time to cover business purchases. The longer the money sits in your bank account, the better off you will be.

REDUCE YOUR NEED FOR INVENTORY

If you run an e-commerce or other retail store, try to avoid keeping inventory. One way to do this is to turn to drop shippers. When you use a drop shipper, you won't have to keep your products in stock or fulfill orders. The drop shipper does. For instance, Jonathan Johnson, the entrepreneur you met in chapter 4 (page 103) who sells riot gear, drop ships about 90% of what he sells. That has helped him grow his two businesses to

$2.8 million in revenue without needing to secure a giant amount of investment capital to stock a warehouse.

KEEP SOME CASH RESERVES

Recent research[8] by the nonprofit organization Prosperity Now, formerly the Corporation for Enterprise Development, on the financial vulnerabilities of microbusiness owners found that 55% of people who owned firms with five employees or fewer said they could cover only a single month's business expenses with their savings—and 30% had no business savings at all. Asked how they would handle an emergency business expense of $1,000, 41% of respondents to an online survey by the nonprofit in the same study said they would have to tap personal savings, and 31% would have to borrow on a personal credit card. Some operated in constant jeopardy: A full 15% said they could not cover such an expense at all. Don't allow yourself to go there. By keeping some emergency funds in reserve, even if that means growing your business more slowly, you can realize your vision for your business—and your lifestyle—no matter what the economy has in store.

---

8 Wiedrich, Kasey. "In Search of Solid Ground: Understanding the Financial Vulnerabilities of Microbusiness Owners." April 2014. Available online at: prosperitynow.org/resources/search-solid-ground-understanding-financial-vulnerabilities-microbusiness-owners-full

USE DIGITAL MARKETING
TO DRIVE DAILY SALES

Generally, there are two ways to use digital marketing. Like Justin Goff, a number of million-dollar entrepreneurs achieve high-volume sales quickly by mastering pay-per-click marketing or other types of digital marketing — or hiring someone who has — to generate a lot of business quickly. But if you turn on the fire hose through digital marketing, make sure you've got the capability to fill the orders you generate or that you can rustle up the money to hire contractors or vendors to help you. Otherwise, your efforts won't produce the potential outcome — and if complaints circulate on social media or the web, you may not get a second chance to earn customers' trust.

CHOOSE ONE: HIGH-VOLUME
SALES OR PREMIUM PRICES

If you don't run the type of business that lends itself to high-volume sales, then you will probably need to find a way to charge premium prices, perhaps by raising your day rate. This approach can work well in professional services firms. One successful coach I interviewed gradually raised his rates over the years. First, he piloted a $10,000-a-day intensive coaching session. When he found there were plenty of takers, he started a year-long coaching program in which he charged clients $250,000 a year. (The clients were affluent entrepreneurs with considerable disposable income.)

Of course, you will be able to charge top-tier rates only if you deliver much better service and results than competitors. You will also need to get in front of customers who not only appreciate what you offer but have the budget to pay your fees.

HIGH PRICE, HIGH PROFIT

Another approach to creating a stable income quickly is selling big-ticket, highly profitable items. That is what Jeffrey J. Rinz, a veteran sales professional, does as an international broker of industrial equipment. Rinz, fifty-eight, spent the early part of his career as a manager and director of international sales in corporate America. But thirty years ago, he got tired of corporate life and started foodWorks, a firm in Cary, North Carolina, that engineers, sells, and installs equipment for large industrial food-processing plants. "I've always admired people who built their own freedom, their own income streams, and are not dependent on other people," he told me. At the time, there was very little social support for making a move like this. "I started out when it wasn't fashionable to work by yourself," says Rinz. "It wasn't that common. Now it is."

Thanks to the commissions he earns by utilizing his sales skills, his company often generates seven-figure revenue, depending on the year. Rinz runs the firm out of his home in the Raleigh area with the help of his wife and a few contractors who work remotely, such as a virtual controller. This father of two sons, one in high school and one in college, says he could never go back to corporate life, given the freedom that comes with this lifestyle.

"I've been able to watch my kids grow," he says. "If my wife and I want to take off on Thursday we do. We don't have to ask permission from a boss." That makes all of the time he put into figuring out the right business model worthwhile.

Remember, your goal is to achieve — and hold onto — financial independence. "There's a sweet spot for every person," says Rinz. "My sweet spot is where I am. It gives me plenty of income, flexibility, and freedom." That's attainable for you, too, if you have the right mindset.

PUT THE RIGHT SYSTEMS IN PLACE FOR GROWTH

Whether you intend to grow your business to the point where it supports your ideal lifestyle or you want to see how far you can take it if you hire a team, you will need to put systems in place to allow you to scale your efforts successfully. The more thought you give to the details when you are starting out, the easier it will be to get your business model right and add to your revenue quickly.

Scott Paladini, thirty-seven, is a master of this. Paladini's father ran Rockaway Bedding, a chain of mattress stores, while he was growing up in New Jersey, and Paladini learned the ropes in a store of his own in Bernardsville, New Jersey, that he no longer owns. But instead of sticking with the conventional product and retail model, Paladini drew on what he absorbed about the industry and created a two-million-dollar business that he runs from a loft in Hoboken. After he hit $2 million, he brought on his first employee and has since added two more. "The business just takes on a life of its own," he says. "You can't be like, 'I only want to sell to two million.'"

Paladini's quest began in 2014, when he began research and development into how to do business online in the mattress industry. He realized there was an opportunity to join the competitive bed-in-a-box industry, where mattresses are compressed into very small boxes and sold online. He studied publications like *PracticalEcommerce* for ideas.

CREATE A SCALABLE PRODUCT OR SERVICE

The trick to competing, Paladini realized, was to create a high-quality, all-foam bed that could be compressed into a small package and shipped inexpensively. Working with a factory in Newnan, Georgia, he developed a mattress that he was confident was comfortable and sturdy enough to attract a steady flow of customers. To make his mattresses more attractive, he covered them with Celliant, a special fiber designed to convert people's natural body heat into far infrared (a range within the spectrum of electromagnetic radiation) energy—which he describes as a light wave with health-promoting properties—notably supporting faster recovery after exercise. "A mattress isn't a commodity," he told me. "At the end of the day, you are spending a lot of your life in your bed."

Launching Bear Mattress two years ago, Paladini focused his marketing on people who have an active lifestyle—a demographic he is part of—and are looking for good muscle recovery at night. Paladini often goes running twice a day and meditates daily. "I love the freedom my business provides," he says.

BUILD MEDIA AND CONSUMER REVIEWS

To get his sales rolling, Paladini sent out samples to mattress review sites, at a cost of about $10,000 for the year. They liked it. One selling point was the pricing. With no overhead for a store or middlemen involved, he was able to keep costs down. A twin mattress is $500, queens are $850, and kings are $950.

Paladini had modest hopes for the business initially. "We thought half a million in sales would be a really good year," he says. But in his first full year in business, sales took off, and he hit $2 million in revenue. How did the mattresses sell so fast? One reason has been customers' raves. Bear Mattress quickly amassed close to one thousand five-star reviews online. Paladini has put an automated system in place to keep them flowing, sending customers emails to invite them to post reviews.

REMOVE BARRIERS TO BUY

But Paladini faced some big obstacles. One was how people shop for mattresses. "People always went to a mattress store to test them," he says. To overcome their fear of buying a mattress they couldn't lie on before handing over their credit card, he put a system in place to ease their apprehension. He gives them a risk-free hundred-day trial, offering a 100% refund if they don't like the mattress, as well as a ten-year warranty. Only a tiny percentage of customers have returned the mattresses, he says. The company donates any returns to local charities or has a mattress-recycling company take them away.

MAKE SALES A PART OF CUSTOMER SERVICE

To stretch what he could do on his own without adding payroll initially, Paladini set up a web-based call center using a provider called Talkdesk to answer customer service calls. "The web-based call center makes it easy to handle customer service from anywhere," Paladini says. "I could be at my beach house and answer customer services calls." Now that he has a well-trained customer service employee on staff, he has delegated answering those calls. The monthly cost of the call center, he says, is minimal.

INVEST IN PUBLIC RELATIONS AND DIGITAL MARKETING

He also hired a public relations firm and a digital marketing team as contractors, to help him spread the word beyond what he could do on his own, and invested in digital radio ads and podcast advertising. Rather than try to become an expert in buying these ads, he relies on a podcast-buying agency. There are many online; ask colleagues in your industry for the name of a good one.

Paladini has now reached the point where his business is growing faster than he ever imagined. But he tries not to get too far ahead of himself. His strategy for success is to ask himself a key question daily: *What can I do to sell more beds today than yesterday?* "You're not going to go from selling one to one thousand overnight," he says. "My goal is to create a longstanding business that adds value to society." By staying focused on creating a sustainable and profitable business, Paladini has been able to avoid many of the common pitfalls of running an ultra-lean startup. Meanwhile, he says, "The brand has grown consistently month over month."

Next, you'll find out how you can navigate some of the traps that can derail entrepreneurs and build a business that you can keep running as long as you want.

5

KEEP GETTING SMARTER

Matt Friel, thirty-two, started playing video games at age five, when his mother got the idea it would sharpen his motor skills, and later, when his family moved from Michigan to Arizona, he found them an ideal refuge from the blazing heat. That started a lifelong passion for gaming. His parents had no idea that his love of Nintendo's Mario games would lead him to run a one-man business that in 2016 brought in $3.6 million in annual revenue. The entrepreneur runs the business from his home near Detroit in Novi, Michigan, where he lives with his wife and their two young children.

Friel came up with the idea for the business, Game Deal Daily, when he was single and living at home with his parents, who had moved the family back to Michigan. Working at video and electronics stores while he earned a bachelor's degree in marketing, Friel noticed that those retailers often put video games on clearance. He thought people who liked classic games that were no longer available in retail stores would buy them on eBay.

It was later, while working on his MBA, that Friel decided the time was right to launch his business. He started purchasing marked-down boxed video games at video and electronic stores in his local area, and then putting them up for sale at higher prices on eBay. He reinvested what he earned in buying more games.

As Friel's sales grew exponentially—from $15,000 his first year to $40,000 in his second and $80,000 in his third—he decided he would take the business full-time when he got his MBA. Getting a conventional job held no appeal for him. Entrepreneurship, in contrast, seemed very attractive, because it enabled him to control his own future. "I never liked the prospect of selling someone else's product so the executives could get rich off of it," he adds. "I don't want to be someone's instrument."

IT'S YOUR BUSINESS LAB

So how did Friel go from making $15,000 a year to more than $3 million? A lot of his success had to do with paying close attention to whether his methods for running the business were working—and using that information to keep his business humming, while protecting the lifestyle he wanted. By constantly seeking improvements to his business and by being willing to do his own research and make frequent changes, he turned each roadblock, wrong turn, and mistake into an opportunity to find a better way to do things—and grow his revenue.

Most million-dollar entrepreneurs turn their businesses into living laboratories from which they can continually learn how to scale their revenue and profits. This isn't something they learn in school (even though some have MBAs). Mostly, they turn to internet research and other entrepreneurs who have a similar mindset to find ways to solve any problems that emerge.

"The key is to ask empowering questions," says Lazlo Nadler, owner of the planner company Tools4Wisdom. In Nadler's view, creating continuous improvement means cultivating purpose-driven curiosity, asking yourself, "How can I grow my business today? What are the top five percent of successful companies implementing today, and how can I implement that, too?"

It's not just a matter of copying and pasting someone else's strategies into your own business plan, Nadler says. He asks himself how he can customize the interesting ideas he comes across. "Often, the answers lead to immediate strategies for my business," he says.

Nadler deployed this mindset in his marketing. Although he doesn't use infomercials to sell his planners, he has found them to be an extraordinary trove of information. He regularly transcribes successful infomercials to study why they are effective and asks himself what's relevant that he can leverage for Tools4Wisdom. He has observed, for example, that "They are not telling you 'buy, buy, buy.' They use highly selective texts."

Noticing that many infomercial scripts include five bullets listing a product's benefits to get customers excited about making a purchase, Nadler includes five bullets in his marketing materials, too. But he has mixed things up by including two questions in the bullets, instead of simple statements. "I try to intrigue the customer," he says.

This way of thinking can help you navigate challenges facing one-person businesses as you try to scale without a lot of overhead.

Here are some of the common obstacles and an inside look at how million-entrepreneurs have met them. As you'll see, there are no cookie-cutter solutions, but there are common thought processes that may help you.

STAY FOCUSED ON THE RIGHT WORK

If your parents, teachers, or past bosses taught you that succeeding depends on hard work and long hours at your desk, unlearning that cubicle-era mindset will be an important step that frees you to create a million-dollar, one-person business. Growing a high-revenue, one-person business is not about chaining yourself to a laptop for twenty hours a day while you live on ultra-caffeinated energy drinks. **It is about working smart and strategically.**

Working smart may sound like obvious advice, but it's easy to forget. In a microbusiness that is growing quickly, small, not-so-efficient tasks—like responding to customers' emails or shipping packages—can mushroom and easily take over all of your waking hours unless you're vigilant. As your startup grows, that will lead to working around the clock and drain the energy you need to think clearly. "It can kind of consume you, if you let it," says Friel.

Friel learned to root out boring time wasters the hard way. As thousands of video game fanatics began discovering his eBay store, he needed to get his hands on a lot more inventory. That was a good problem to have. But finding the video games started taking up an unsustainable amount of time. "There were days I would drive around for ten or twelve hours," says Friel. Eventually, he got worn down and realized he'd taken this method as far as

ELIMINATE, AUTOMATE, DELEGATE, PROCRASTINATE

To keep his mind and schedule clear, Nadler uses an approach he calls Eliminate, Automate, Delegate, Procrastinate. He hunts continually for new ways to avoid doing things that don't matter, to automate repetitive and labor-intensive processes, and to outsource work to contractors. "There are so many distractions that pull us away," he says.

That means being honest with himself about how he is spending his time. "I have a funnel where I do an analysis of what my workflow looks like," says Nadler. Here are the questions he asks himself:

- What can I eliminate?
- What can I outsource?
- What can I put on the back burner?
- What can I say "no" to?

This approach can work for you, too. The key is to be disciplined about acting on your answers.

it could go. "You can't really scale a business that way unless you want to live out of your car."

Often the answer to situations like this is research—which will cost you time but not money. Instead of resigning himself to fighting traffic in Detroit or hiring someone else to do the same inefficient task, Friel began searching the internet for ideas on finding inventory more efficiently. Using LinkedIn, he eventually reached out to some of the major video game sellers on eBay for advice. In doing so, he learned that some of them were also distributors. He began buying his games from them at a bulk discount, freeing himself from hours in the car. That allowed him to regain his focus on growing his business.

Friel took the same approach to shipping his games. During the first few years that he ran the business, he packed up and shipped every order himself. It was boring, but he powered through it and got it done quickly. That changed as hundreds of customers started placing orders. Shipping began eating up all of his time—especially around the December holidays, when he does about half of his sales.

"It just got crazy," says Friel. "I would get over a thousand orders a day. I was wearing my wife down. I would wake up and work until I went to bed. I was working seventeen-hour days trying to fill all of my orders during the holidays."

Friel didn't know how to fix the situation without letting his customers down, so he began researching other options on the internet. That led him to move his store from eBay to a giant e-commerce site and to switch to a fulfillment service run by that mega site. Friel now ships his inventory to a warehouse run by the huge online site, which fills his orders for most of his sales. The site, in turn, takes about a 35% share of the revenue from each sale.

"It's a pretty big cut," says Friel. But he sees many benefits. "It's a lot less manual labor for me, and they promote you more if you store your stuff in their warehouses and allow them to fill the orders for you," he says. Plus, by keeping some of his inventory in the e-commerce site's warehouses, he has more room to store inventory in his own local three-thousand-square-foot warehouse, eliminating the need to rent more warehouse space — a substantial savings.

But there is still work Friel must do before he ships his products. To put any needed packaging and barcodes on his products — something he also did manually at first — he relies on Cassell and Associates, an occupational health service that hires brain injury survivors to do this work as they recover. "That used to be something that would take a lot of my time — doing repetitive processes that don't utilize my more unique skills," says Friel.

Without tasks like this clogging up his schedule, Friel has plenty of time to play with his children, compete in a soccer league with his wife, and shoot hoops with his friends twice a week — activities that recharge him. Although he still loves video games, he plays only once or twice a month. Decompressing far from a computer screen gives him the distance he needs to keep improving the business — and he and his family can enjoy the freedom that comes with making a great living.

There are many creative ways to squeeze mundane time wasters out of your business—and new solutions are coming out constantly. In a million-dollar, one-person business, there is no single right way to do things. What works for other entrepreneurs may not work for you, so always prioritize researching tools that will help you be most efficient.

Persistence paid off for Allen Walton, the owner of SpyGuy. Like Friel, Walton also found that shipping took a lot of his time in his first year. Through research, he uncovered an online service, ShippingEasy, which took that burden off of him. When someone places an order on Walton's website, the site automatically sends the order to ShippingEasy. ShippingEasy then notifies his suppliers of the order. Because Walton has programmed all of his products' weights and sizes into ShippingEasy, these vendors can put the item in the right size box. ShippingEasy automatically generates a shipping label and postage so they can send it to Walton's customers. By eliminating work that he or an employee would have to do, Walton has freed time and money he can devote to growth.

"I want to become a $10 million company," says Walton. "I need to spend time on the activities where I can grow my business exponentially."

FIND HELP YOU CAN TRUST

No matter how good you are at winning new business, your growth will stall if you don't build the right team. It doesn't necessarily matter whether you opt for contractors or outside vendors. What is important is that you find ones you can trust to do a great job and help you grow your business.

Nadler hunts continually for new ways to outsource work to contractors and to automate repetitive and labor-intensive

STAY INSPIRED

One way to avoid getting lost in the mundane aspects of running a business is to keep yourself in touch with your higher purpose in life. To fuel his creativity, stay inspired, and remain connected to why he is doing what he does, Nadler, like many million-dollar entrepreneurs, reads voraciously.

Here are some of Nadler's favorite books and sources of inspiration:

Essentialism (Crown Business, 2014)
by Greg McKeown

"Essentialism helps transform your focus from trying to achieve it all to picking your top 5% and shelving the rest until you accomplish your number one priority."

Man's Search for Meaning (Beacon Press, 2006)
by Viktor Frankl

"Frankl is an Auschwitz survivor who lost everything and [out of that experience] came up with logotherapy, [a form of therapy based on the belief that says the search for meaning is the most powerful human driver]. When you have a strong enough 'why' in your life, any 'how' is justified."

Brain Pickings (brainpickings.org)

Nadler finds constant creative inspiration in this "interestingness digest," which covers art, poetry, science, and other topics far from the business world.

processes. There are plenty of online platforms, such as Upwork and Freelancer.com, where you can find these contractors and try them out on a small engagement, to see if you like the quality of their work and they can meet your other requirements, such as delivering projects on time. Or you can just look for talent in the circle of people you know and meet. When Nadler was out to dinner with his brother one evening, for instance, he identified a woman who could be the model he needed for the lifestyle photos on his website.

The same holds true with outside vendors. To evaluate his web copy and design, Nadler turned to a site called Splitly to do his A/B testing for consumer preferences. This saves him hours of manual work. Nadler has found the site's small team offers smart insights to the questions he is trying to answer. "The size of your company doesn't matter when you have the right brains," he notes.

A/B TESTING 101

If you run a business that depends on online customers, it is important to know, to the best of your ability, what makes them click on particular pages and links on your site and do what you want them to do, whether that is to buy, subscribe, or participate in your social media campaign by sending in a photograph. Your gut instincts may not always be right about what people actually respond to. Asking visitors directly what they like and don't like may be equally unhelpful. Visitors may not be candid if, for instance, they'd be embarrassed to admit to some of the material they tend to click on.

Your website's analytics tools will allow you to determine which pages on your site are the most popular, what actions visitors take on your site, or what paths they follow—all of which can be immensely valuable. Sometimes, though, you may to get a jump-start by getting information about how they are responding to a new design you are considering.

That is when A/B testing comes in. In A/B testing, you can, for instance, create two versions of a page you plan to post, run them past your target audience, and find out which one performed best. You essentially divide up the traffic between the two designs.

There are many tools for A/B testing. Nadler likes Splitly (splitly.com). Other options include Optimizely (optimizely.com), VWO (vwo.com), and Google Analytics Content Experiments (https://support .google.com/analytics/answer/1745147), part of Google Analytics. Try several options—often there are free trials—before you commit. Your A/B testing tool will only help you *if you actually use it*, so unless you're a techie, the best tool may be the one that's easiest and most intuitive for you.

When you hand off the work, it's important to keep a close eye on how vendors are performing. If they don't deliver, your business will suffer—and your customers may not cut you much slack. Ask Justin Goff, the ebook entrepreneur from chapter 3 (page 86). In addition to his info-marketing company—which, as you may recall, sold a military-inspired exercise plan—he created a second million-dollar business. That startup, an online health supplements store called Patriot Health Institute, sold men supplements to help them feel more energetic.

By using Facebook marketing to promote the business, Goff built the profitable solo operation to $1 million in revenue in a year. A third-party fulfillment center shipped the orders for him. But Goff ended up selling the business a year after he launched it, as it became too hard to keep up with customer service. When I searched for Patriot Health Institute online, I noticed there were several complaints online and asked him what had happened. He responded candidly: "One of our biggest issues, when we were growing, was we were really good at acquiring new customers and making good products they liked. Our biggest problem was customer service. We tried to do all of our customer service by email at the time, which later we realized was a mistake. Our market was mostly people in their fifties, sixties, and seventies. A huge part of that market wants to talk to someone over the phone." Although the company later offered phone support, handled by a third party, he concluded that its service could have been improved, too.

Goff's original goal was to keep his business as small and lean as possible, but, he says, "in this situation, it definitely backfired a little." He estimates that out of about forty thousand sales, the business received about seven to ten complaints. "In the overall scheme of things, our complaints were super low." However, online posts can affect business down the line.

The experience provided a valuable lesson. Goff realized that while he was a good copywriter and knew how to attract people to his website and convert them to customers, he needed to learn more about operations and finding the right talent.

Goff became a silent partner in a bigger supplement firm that already had the support and talent he needed in place. "If I wanted to build this into a hugely successful supplement company, I needed infrastructure and people to help me do it," he says.

Goff has since moved on to new challenges. He sold his stake in the supplement business when the other owners made an attractive offer so they could own all of the shares. He moved to Austin, Texas, where entrepreneurship is percolating, to look for his next opportunity. "I'm sure I'm going to be onto something else," says Goff. "I'm not exactly sure what yet." It is all part of the learning process for this serial entrepreneur, who keeps finding ways to expand his knowledge and get better at what he does.

6

REALIZE AND RESET
YOUR VISION

When Katherine Krug raised money on Kickstarter to manufacture her BetterBack posture-support device, it was just the beginning of her success. She soon appeared on the TV show *Shark Tank*, where entrepreneurs pitch their ideas to investors to raise cash, but she decided not to take the investment capital that was offered to her. Nonetheless, the publicity helped her business grow. All told, in her first 365 days of business, Krug brought in $3 million in revenue. She's now working on a next-generation product.

As Krug has grown the business, she has had to answer an important question: "What is my vision for BetterBack — and my life — and how do I achieve it?" For some entrepreneurs in fast-growing one-person startups, that vision is to keep expanding until their business morphs into a traditional, job-creating business that dominates a niche in its industry. For others, it is to build a boutique business that is the best at what it does but has no employees. For still others, there are many hybrid versions of these two models.

The beauty of owning a microbusiness is that you are free to choose the route that is best for you. When you make decisions about your path, you are not beholden to anyone, other than your family, if you have one, or, in some cases, your investors.

Still, it can be tough to exercise that freedom. As human beings, even very independent ones, we care what other people think. If you travel in circles of those who believe creating the next billion-dollar company is the only worthy pursuit for an entrepreneur, and your dream is to keep your business ultra-lean and your lifestyle very flexible, you may not get much reinforcement or respect for doing things your way.

That can be discouraging, but it doesn't mean you should try to force yourself into the mold of Mark Zuckerberg or Elon Musk and try to like it, if you want something different. Giving some conscious thought to what you really want and pursuing your own personal vision will be more rewarding.

The happiest million-dollar entrepreneurs tend to do three things to realize their vision: First, they take their entrepreneurial temperature frequently, asking themselves what they want to achieve in the business and if their efforts are leading in that direction—and frequently revising their answers to fit changing circumstances. Second, they set clear goals and stay true to them, until it makes sense to refresh them. And finally, they are prepared to reinvest in their business, or other pursuits, when the timing is right. Here is how they pull it off.

RETAKE YOUR
ENTREPRENEURIAL TEMPERATURE

Most million-dollar entrepreneurs take time away from the daily details of their businesses to consciously think about their vision for the business, assess whether they are realizing it, and course-correct if they are not. That is not easy to do in a microbusiness, where it's hard to keep up with the tasks you need to accomplish each day. Nonetheless, stepping aside to do some strategic thinking will separate you from people who stay on a treadmill and never grow their revenue much.

Krug—who speaks at the rapid pace of someone who can't wait to dive into her day—does not have much time each day to ponder her vision. So, to stay in what she calls "expansion/contraction mode"—which means she continually expands her business while also stepping back from the chaos to observe what is going on—she blocks out a few minutes every morning to think and reflect. When she wakes up, she and her husband, Jonathan Swanson, a fellow entrepreneur who cofounded the on-demand platform Thumbtack, do a meditation exercise called Grow. In the exercise, they each name one thing they are grateful for, share one thing they regret and would like to do better, mention one opportunity they want to go after and express wonder, by asking themselves: What is one thing I am amazed at and in awe of? Doing this simple exercise has helped her surface what really matters to her and stay focused on her vision day after day.

In the course of doing this type of thinking, Krug realized she wanted to keep growing her business at a fast pace—but wants to keep the freedom to live the way she wants. That means not running a traditional office where she would have to supervise employees. Although Krug often works around the clock, she likes to live a mobile lifestyle, where at any given time she may be working from Tokyo, Sundance, or a pool in Miami.

It took Krug a while to get clear on what she wanted. As her sales took off, she wondered if it was time to put some core employees on payroll, as many other companies do. She knew from her days as an employee that working under one roof brought a "social glue" that was hard to create another way. But when Krug tried hiring her own employee to help her for a ninety-day trial period, she quickly found the situation frustrating. "She started taking on every little project, and nothing really crossed the finish line," Krug says with a sigh. "If it did, it was done in a way that was not creative."

Krug could have trained her employee more or looked for someone else, but the traditional boss-employee relationship just didn't feel right to her. Plus, she chafes at the administrative aspects of running an office. "There's so much overhead and so many more meetings," she says.

Ultimately, Krug opted to continue relying on contractors to help her grow, as she has done successfully from the beginning. She found that she was energized by working with contractors and consultants, such as the product design specialists who helped her create her product. They were self-motivated, because of their own desire to build a successful business, as well as loyal.

When she hires contractors, she noted, "It's about getting the job done. We have fun together. If someone stops doing an amazing job, you part ways amicably."

Even with her business growing rapidly, she has not had to change a lifestyle she loves, because of her conscious decision to run the firm the way that works for her. "I have tried to structure the business exactly in a way that fits my life and goals, which is to have the most impact possible," says Krug. "By impact, I mean really helping customers with the smallest number of people on the team—which creates flexibility in my life." To avoid overwork, she is planning to grow by expanding the pool of contractors she uses.

Jason Weisenthal, who is in his forties, took a very different route when deciding how to grow his e-commerce business, WallMonkeys. His business, based in Gaithersburg, Maryland, prints giant wall decals made from photos of kids playing sports, which families use to decorate the children's rooms. A former shoe-store owner, Weisenthal opened the business in his basement after closing the store during the recession. As WallMonkeys took off and hit seven-figure revenues, Weisenthal opened a print-on-demand facility and warehouse. To staff the business, he has had as many as five employees on his payroll at certain times. For technical projects, he still hires contractors. "You have to do that globally," says Weisenthal. "If you limit yourself to a region you are looking at such a smaller talent pool."

For Weisenthal, attending events with other entrepreneurs and joining The Brotherhood, a Facebook peer group, has helped him make the right decisions about how to grow his business. "Being able to bounce questions off each other and share information with like-minded intelligent people is very important," he says.

Weisenthal has also been able to draw on the wisdom of many entrepreneurial friends through a by-application-only annual event called MastermindTalks. The event brings together a carefully selected group of entrepreneurs in settings like the Napa Valley, California. "There's nobody in my town that I really feel like I connect with like that," says Weisenthal. "When you go to these events it's like food for your soul."

Krug and Weisenthal made very different decisions about how to move forward with their companies, but they came to the same realization: **Running a business as a solo operation isn't an end in itself. It isn't a religion to which you have to pledge lifetime devotion. It's a way of supporting your vision for making a great living and living the way you want.** How they were alike was staying open to altering their course and finding a better way.

For many solo entrepreneurs, there may come a point when, if demand grows enough, they need to commit to a different way of scaling. That may be through automation, hiring contractors, outsourcing, or putting people on payroll. What matters in the end is finding a way to run your business that makes you happy, without mistreating anyone.

STAY TRUE TO YOUR EVOLVING GOALS

The more successful your business becomes, the more people will be inclined to give you advice on what to do next. **We can all learn from others' wisdom, but if you've created a vision and goals that work for you, it is important to be selective in the advice you listen to.**

Jayson Gaignard, thirty-two, founded and runs MastermindTalks, the Toronto-based firm that produces the three-day events that have been so helpful to Weisenthal.

MastermindTalks—which Gaignard runs with some help from his wife and an assistant who is a contractor—could easily expand. About four thousand to five thousand people apply annually to attend the event for 150 entrepreneurs, which features well-known speakers such as Tim Ferriss, and costs $10,000 to attend. Gaignard is a natural connector and an early adopter of practices like sending video introductions via email.

Given the success of MastermindTalks, there are many ways Gaignard could grow it, such as adding more attendees, holding the event more frequently, or charging more to attend—and many people have suggested these. Gaignard isn't closed to these ideas, but he has decided not to pursue them. He raised the cost of attending the event early on. One time he tried expanding it to 160 people, but felt the gathering was a little too large and shrank it back down again. Gaignard ultimately decided he wants to deliver an unforgettable experience, where he can control details like frequent seating rotations. "If it's a great experience, I won't have to do any marketing," says Gaignard. That has meant sticking with what already works.

Gaignard's decision to keep the business as is goes beyond quality control. It also makes better financial sense to him than creating a mega-event. At an earlier business he ran, the ticket retailer TicketsCanada, Gaignard assumed when he hit $1.5 million in revenue that he would double his $350,000 in profits if he could hit $3 million. What he didn't anticipate was that higher overhead would prevent the expected growth in profits. "I had to almost double my staff and get a larger office space," he says. In fact, when his revenue hit $3 million, his profits reached only $400,000. Although his revenue eventually grew to $7 million, he had to bring almost twenty people on staff to achieve that and saw a similarly incremental gain in profits.

After this experience, with MastermindTalks Gaignard decided to do things differently. The business currently brings in $1.7 million in annual revenue through its conference and a couple of smaller retreats, which he plans to phase out. "We decided to strip back the business and focus on what we're really good at," says Gaignard. He achieves close to a 40% profit on this revenue and is very happy with that.

He concludes, "We're at a point now where we're very successful. Everyone is saying we've got to scale. I say, 'What is the need?' I pay myself about $250,000 a year, and a lot of the money stays in the business for reinvestment. How much more money do I need?"

DODGE DISTRACTIONS

Distractions will be one of the biggest enemies of achieving your personal vision for your business. Constantly chasing new opportunities—an occupational hazard for entrepreneurs—can keep you from accomplishing anything of substance, notes BetterBack founder Katherine Krug.

She's observed that "People spend too much time trying to chase down seemingly exciting opportunities as opposed to the highest leverage thing they can do for their business. By only doing a couple of things really well, we've been able to do really well."

When Krug has trouble resisting new opportunities, she asks herself these exploratory questions to clarify whether she should move forward:

- Is this one of the highest-impact things I could do for my business?
- Would waiting six months to do this negatively impact the business?
- Would I be missing out on the opportunity altogether if I waited six months to try this?

"If the answer to these questions is "no," I'll punt it for six months," she says.

JUST SAY "NO"

Learning how to take a pass on interesting opportunities that may distract you from your vision and goals is the most critical skill you can develop if you want to grow revenue exponentially at an ultra-lean business. Adam Bornstein, thirty-four, and his brother Jordan, twenty-six, know this well.

Based in Denver, Colorado, the brothers have created two seven-figure businesses built around their passions. One is Born Fitness, a business that offers nutrition coaching. The other is Pen Name Consulting, which provides branding and strategic advice on growth involving editorial, social media, and podcast production, to high-profile clients such as Tim Ferriss, Arnold Schwarzenegger, Equinox Fitness, and other clients. Both of the Bornsteins' businesses have lean teams. Born Fitness has five employees. At Pen Name Consulting, the brothers are the only permanent staff; they pull in expert contractors when they need to.

The Bornstein brothers have many opportunities to grow Pen Name Consulting, where they work with only two or three "executive" clients at a time. But to stay true to their vision, they have learned to say "No" to any who are not their ideal customers.

"Growth is often viewed by how many more clients you can take on," says Adam. "For us, it's measured by how much can we help our clients. I want to be judged by success. I don't want any of our clients to fail. The best marketing is just doing a really freaking awesome job at everything you do."

That does not mean they want to keep the business where it is. To grow revenues, the brothers hold high-end business retreats, called two12, once or twice a year. While the events do take planning, the brothers keep them small and intimate—limiting the application-only event to sixty-five people—which prevents organizing the events from taking over their lives.

WHAT TO DO WHEN GROWTH STALLS

If your vision is to create a $1 million business and your revenues are stuck, consider bringing in a mentor or coach to help you think through what is blocking you. Adam Bornstein hired a coach, Noah Kagan, after getting Born Fitness to the $500,000 in revenue mark but having trouble nudging it up to $1 million. Kagan, an early Facebook employee, is an entrepreneur who founded a newsletter for startups now known as Sumo.

"Noah came to me with a very simple question: What do I do best within my business—and how I could do that even better?" Bornstein recalls.

Bornstein originally thought that providing unique, highly personalized coaching was what he did best, but he couldn't figure out how to do more of that than he already was. Then, through his discussions with Kagan, he realized that his ego was getting in the way. What kept customers coming to the business was that they got highly personalized coaching, but they didn't necessarily need him to be the coach.

Determined to bring in $1 million annually, Bornstein began training other coaches to use his methods and expanded the business to five traditional employees. "I had to make a decision to hire people, teach them to do what I do, and do overkill to make sure they gave the same type of TLC I gave people," says Bornstein.

That took patience, but he eventually created a system in which every client gets separate coaches in three areas: fitness, nutrition, and lifestyle/accountability. This led to higher client satisfaction, a better growth rate, and frequent renewals. "Getting someone's money is not the ultimate goal," says Bornstein. "It is keeping them very satisfied, so they will continue investing in me." That, in turn, has helped him generate annual revenue above $1 million and have a profitable company.

Bornstein isn't the only entrepreneur I spoke with who has invested money in hiring a coach to help them avoid distractions. When Jason Weisenthal found himself struggling with procrastination on new initiatives and spending too much time on minutia, such as answering text messages, he asked contacts he met through the events he attends for a referral to a coach. The same name kept coming up—and it was someone he knew. "He is an e-commerce person who has grown his business bigger than mine," says Weisenthal. "I swallowed my pride a bit and hired him."

Weisenthal's focus is better since he began working with his coach. "I was doing too many different things and not completing enough," says Weisenthal. "I needed help moving onto one thing at a time. He's helped me a lot."

MANAGE YOUR FINANCES WISELY: Q&A WITH RICK EDELMAN

Once your business achieves high revenue, it will ideally help you pay for the lifestyle you want, but you have to manage the financial realities of self-employment wisely. This requires a conscious effort and, often, professional advice.

The well-known financial advisor Rick Edelman, author of *The Truth About Your Future*, which discusses how both people in traditional jobs and the self-employed can navigate some common challenges, has some valuable suggestions. His approach to investing is a multipronged one, built on diversifying investments, maintaining a long-term focus, doing strategic rebalancing, and investing in exponential technologies. As someone who is self-employed himself, he understands the realities many entrepreneurs face.

Many people are now participating in the freelance economy, whether voluntarily or involuntarily. What is the number one piece of financial advice you would give them?

Edelman: The primary difference is that your financial security is entirely dependent on you. Most people are unaware that when you are working for a big company only 60% of compensation is salary. The other 40% is in the form of noncash compensation: insurance benefits, paid time off, 401(k) contributions, and the like. As a self-employed individual, you don't enjoy any of those benefits. If you mow lawns, the homeowner is going to pay you to mow the lawn but isn't going to put money into your IRA. As a result, you have to make sure that your compensation, which is entirely cash, is enough to compensate for the absence of employer-provided benefits.

Should self-employed people and small-business owners invest differently from traditional employees, and if so, how?

Edelman: They should invest the way I describe in the book *The Truth About Your Future*. The advice I give on how everyone should be saving for their future is applicable regardless of the nature of your employment or your job income. If you are going to succeed in business, you have to have certain traits. Number one: you must be agile. Opportunities present themselves suddenly. Changes in the marketplace occur without notice—changes in competition, changes in technology, regulation, pricing. You have to be able to adapt very rapidly to maintain your competitive edge.

However, if you are going to be agile in investing, it means you are going to be a market timer. You will constantly jump in and out of stocks. That kind of active trading never succeeds. The entrepreneur who wants to constantly go with the flow—that will hurt him with his investment strategy.

The second trait of the entrepreneur is concentration. Entrepreneurs know they must concentrate all of their resources—time and money—in their business. But if you apply that same approach to your investments and concentrate your funds in a single stock, the concentration risk will destroy you. You should own a basket of hundreds of stocks.

Entrepreneurs often have to be on guard against their own nature in their investment portfolio. Don't trade too often.

One recent survey by accounting software provider FreshBooks found that many entrepreneurs don't have retirement accounts, even at age fifty. How can they get started on saving now, even if they've put it off?

Edelman: It depends on how much money they want to contribute and how confident they are they will continue contributing year after year. The simplest, easiest, and quickest is a SEP IRA. This can be created any time. It's very flexible, very fluid year to year. (In recent years, IRS guidelines allowed contributions up to 25% of one's compensation or [up to] $54,000.) If you wanted to tuck away even more than that, there are other types of retirement plans that allow you to contribute more money. They come with the obligation to contribute every year. The simplest solution is to go to an independent financial advisor familiar with retirement plans for self-employed people and small business owners.

For many self-employed people, high taxes are a big obstacle to saving. Finding a good accountant can help, but what other steps can they take to reduce their tax burden?

Edelman: One of the great things about America is that it was founded by capitalists. Our tax code has always had a bias in favor of entrepreneurs. The tax code offers a large array of deductions and credits for people building businesses. I've discovered that many small business owners are not taking advantage of all of the deductions available to them, such as the retirement plan we just talked about, deductions for business expenses, and depreciation schedules for equipment they purchase. There are a wide variety of deductions. It is important to become familiar with the tax codes or hire a professional tax advisor who can give guidance.

Health care can be very costly to buy independently, and in the current US environment it is an unpredictable cost. For people who don't have access to tax subsidies or a spouse's health plan, do you have any recommendations for keeping costs in check?

Edelman: Unfortunately, no. This is why health care is one of the dominant social issues in our nation. There is no effective answer for business owners other than to recognize they do need to acknowledge the importance of this and factor it into their pricing. A mistake that young entrepreneurs make is offering their services at lower rates than their competition. They feel their overhead is lower so they can afford to charge less. They often fail to consider their higher tax liability and insurance and retirement needs. It is a very rare business owner who can succeed for long by using price as a value proposition.

For self-employed people, saving for their children's college expenses can be challenging. Any advice?

Edelman: When filling out the Free Application for Federal Student Aid (FAFSA), you've got to be very, very careful to provide accurate information so the admissions officer understands the nature of your income. Otherwise the officer can assign you a higher income than you actually have.

KNOW WHEN TO REINVEST— AND WHEN NOT TO

One of the most exciting parts of building a successful business is having the opportunity to take it as far as you want. In some cases, it may make sense to put more money into your business to reach more customers. That is what Katherine Krug is doing after listening to the feedback from her customers at BetterBack on how to make her invention better and adding new features, like enabling people to use heat or ice to soothe their backs while on the go. "It's really about how can you do something differently from other people," she says. "How can you find a way that can achieve growth, distribution, and scale in a way that no one else is doing or only a few people know about?"

Hal Elrod, thirty-eight, took a similar approach to his writing business. When the former salesman wrote and published a self-help book called *The Miracle Morning* about techniques that helped him change his life after a car crash almost took his life, it became a runaway hit on a major internet bookstore, thanks to efforts like a podcast he ran to promote it and live events he holds to bring together readers. *The Miracle Morning* has now been translated into twenty-four languages. "Writing doesn't come naturally to me," he admits. "It took me three years." By his second year of selling it, his annual revenue had hit more than $500,000. As it began to approach $1 million, he hired an assistant to help him run his business. By his third year of selling the book, revenue had reached $1.5 million per year, and his profits were high. In year four, revenue reached $2.4 million.

Excited about the enthusiasm for the book, Elrod reinvested in his brand and has released ten Miracle Morning books in the series, including companion guides. He now has seven revenue streams, ranging from his books and keynote speaking events to private coaching and consulting, and he is enjoying transitioning to running a larger enterprise.

"I'm going from being a solopreneur my whole career to needing more of a team," he says. "I'm partnering with people who have programs or products I really believe in that I feel would really benefit my community."

In one such partnership, he has teamed up for the last three years with John Berghoff, cofounder and managing partner of the Flourishing Leadership Institute, to run a live event called the Best Year Ever Blueprint. "I didn't have the experience running multiyear, interactive experiential events," says Elrod. Berghoff, in contrast, had run many such gatherings around the world.

"We partnered on the first event, and it went off great, combining his strengths and my strengths," says Elrod. "That is one of the keys to a successful partnership—making sure your values are aligned and, once you have, looking at how your strengths complement each other's."

If you decide you'd rather run a small, boutique business, however, it may not make sense to pour more money into it than you already have and invest in ventures like Elrod's. Because Jayson Gaignard wants to keep his MastermindTalks business at the size it is, he has decided to reinvest his profits in a new project: focusing on helping other entrepreneurs grow their businesses as a consultant. He sees this new venture as one that will flow naturally from what he is already doing. "I know my skill set and the Rolodex I have," he says. "I'm very good at starting businesses. My expertise is in taking them from zero to seven figures very quickly."

No doubt, not all of the ventures you read about in this book will turn out the way the founders intended or expected. Some may close or fail. Some owners may sell. But many will continue to succeed, either as solo entrepreneurs or in businesses that expand to include a team of employees. And embracing this lifestyle is only going to get easier, given the fast-growing community of people who are mastering the nuances of building high-revenue, ultra-lean businesses that allow them to live the way they want. The entrepreneurs who shared their stories in this book have been generous in explaining exactly what has helped them to get there. Are you ready to join them? Then today is the day to get moving and take the first steps.

APPENDICES

Congratulations on completing this crash course in starting and running a million-dollar, one-person business. I hope you feel more prepared to create your own high-revenue, ultra-lean business. It can be a brand-new career path, no matter what changes transform the economy in the future.

Running a million-dollar, one-person business isn't just a matter of hitting a revenue benchmark. After all, for one person, hitting $1 million may be the practical equivalent of another person's reaching $250,000; it depends on your financial responsibilities and lifestyle goals. This book is about a brand-new outlook on running a business, one that is realistic about what it costs to live and offers a way to rise above the constant, grinding economic stress that engulfs many self-employed people, without giving up control over your time. It is a fresh way of looking at work, one where you determine your personal priorities and design a business that supports them, and you, in a healthy way. Those priorities will no doubt evolve as your life changes. There may be some times when you choose to be more energetic about growing your revenue and profits than others.

If you truly embrace what you've learned here and apply the lessons of the entrepreneurs who have shared their ideas, you will open exciting new possibilities in your life that you may never have envisioned before. You will not have to worry about a day when robots take over your job and your only alternative is to live on a "basic income." You will always have much better options—for which you, alone, are the decision maker. You will not have to wait for an external gatekeeper to give you permission to pursue them.

Like anything worth doing, starting a million-dollar, one-person business requires careful thought and soul searching. It's not easy to come up with a great idea for a new product or service, and it's even more challenging to turn it into an ultra-lean business that you can scale to seven-figure revenue. Reading about successful entrepreneurs can help you learn how to do that, but in the end, you've got to act on what *you* know and learn—or nothing will happen.

Fortunately, if you set aside some time to complete the following worksheets, you can jump-start your progress. They will help you get clear on what you really want out of your business, beyond a doubt—and build the momentum you need to achieve your goals.

WHAT REALLY MATTERS?

The ideal million-dollar, one-person business will allow you to achieve both your revenue and profit targets and the lifestyle goals that matter most to you. Here are some questions to ponder. As you write down or think through your responses, you'll gain clarity on what matters most to you when starting a business.

What do I like about my current way of making a living or my economic situation?

Am I willing to leave behind what I like most about my current way of making a living or economic situation to start a business?

Is what I like most about my current way of making a living or economic situation likely to be available to me in the next three to five years? What about in the next ten years?

What would I like to change about my current income or economic situation?

Would I be able to change the things I dislike about my current income or economic situation by running my own business?

Would the business I want to start allow me to spend more of my time doing things I enjoy?

Would the business I want to start force me to spend a lot of time on things I don't like?

Would the business I want to start require me to do things I'm generally not willing to do, am not good at, and don't think I can learn? If so, is there any way around that?

Am I getting the professional rewards I want from my current work?

Would running a business help me achieve my professional goals in a way that my current pursuits don't allow?

Am I getting the personal rewards I desire, such as friendships with interesting people, from the work I do now?

Would I be able to improve my personal life by running a business?

Am I happy with the way I'm spending my time, most days?

Are the hours I am spending on my key pursuits commensurate with how much they matter to me?

If there are imbalances in how I'm spending my time, am I frustrated by them?

Would the businesses that most interest me realistically allow me to fix any imbalances that bother me?

Would the business I want to start interfere with good things that I have in my life now, such as time to spend with friends or time with my children?

If so, how would I deal with that? Are there any adaptations I could make to the business to prevent losing things that matter to me?

If I had to choose, what are the one or two things that I really hope to get from starting a business?

Will the businesses I am considering allow me to achieve those things in a time span I consider reasonable?

If it will take a long time to achieve the one or two things I really want, will I have the patience and resources to stick it out?

DEFINING YOUR EXPERTISE

Many budding entrepreneurs think they can succeed only in marketing expertise that is tied to what they studied in school or do for a living. Those avenues can offer you exciting possibilities, but there may be many more options available to you.

Once you find an idea, be honest with yourself about whether you are able and willing to execute it. "You can say, 'I'd love to make gluten-free food,' but if you're not determined and don't know how to cook, it's not the right business," says Debra Cohen, a million-dollar home improvement entrepreneur. "People contact me all the time and say, 'I love your business idea. You work from home. I want to do that, too'—but if you're not a people person or a creative thinker, my business isn't going to work. It has to be something that resonates with you and matches your skill set. You have to be aware of what you are willing to invest, personally and professionally. It really is a lot of work. You have to be willing to make the commitment and sacrifices that are necessary."

These questions will help you tease out your unique genius or marketable expertise:

What niche areas of your work do you have a special passion for—and a deep knowledge about?

What hobbies and personal interests do you read and learn about constantly, because you genuinely enjoy them?

Which of your endeavors generate the most curiosity among the people you meet? These may be activities like home-schooling, urban farming, teaching abroad, or other pursuits the average person may not have had a chance to try.

What challenges and problems have you addressed success-fully in your own unique way after doing thorough research? These may be "good" problems like decorating a small house on a budget, or serious ones, like addressing a child's illness through alternative healing modalities.

What roles do you play in your personal life—parent, care-giver, coach, neighbor, mentor, volunteer—that have given you unique knowledge that might benefit others?

What situations have you been unwittingly thrust into that gave you a fresh perspective on an issue people care about?

What trends do you know about that other people have yet to discover?

BUSINESS IDEA BRAINSTORM

Some people have dozens of business ideas. Others don't think they have any. The trick to starting a million-dollar, one-person business is identifying an idea you love that has the ability to generate high revenue and profits on an initial shoestring. As explained early in this book, uncovering this type of business is different from finding a business that is a job substitute—though if you create a business in which you can amplify your own efforts and generate high revenue, you will create a great alternative to a traditional job along the way.

Here's a guided exercise to help you uncover your million-dollar, one-person business. Once you come up with your idea, you'll be ready to put it to the test on a small scale to see if it is something customers will pay for.

What interests am I most passionate about? Are there any interests I am so obsessive about that only other fellow fanatics can relate, or in which I have developed a rare or unusual expertise?

What interests do I enjoy thinking about every day, even if they are not burning passions?

What types of work do I most enjoy in my daily life, whether it's in the course of taking care of household responsibilities, working in a paid job, volunteering, or recreation?

In which areas do objective people—particularly those who are not close family members and friends—tell me I have exceptional skill, experience, or proficiency?

In what areas of interest do I lack marketable skills, experience, or proficiencies that I could monetize but have a strong commitment to developing—and the means to access any necessary education in a short time span?

Which of these interests would I enjoy even more by turning them into a business?

Which of these interests would I enjoy much less if I tried to make money from them?

In which of the areas I enjoy do I have skills, experience, proficiencies, or the capability to produce products or services I could potentially make money from?

After asking myself all of these questions, what top three types of one-person businesses would I be most excited about running and, realistically, be most likely to be able to start?

Among these top three, which type of business has the greatest potential to allow me to multiply my efforts as a single individual without hiring employees at the outset? Which one would allow me to use contractors, outsourcing, automation, or other resource-stretchers most effectively, so making more isn't dependent on my simply working more hours?

MARKET RESEARCH
CRASH COURSE

If you launch a business in the industry in which you already work, you will have a head start on your market research. Knowing what is going on in an industry and understanding where there are gaps in the marketplace will give you an edge.

The same holds true if you are a consumer of the type of product you plan to sell. If, for instance, you're a parent and have scoured the internet for a children's product that you really need — but no one makes it — all of that digging is valuable market research, too.

But it is important to expand your research beyond your individual knowledge. There is always more to the story. In an ever-more-connected world, changes happening a continent away could upend your plans if you are not prepared. Here are some tools to tap to make sure you know there is a future market — and how big and sustainable that market is — for what you want to sell.

GIANT E-COMMERCE SITES

Sort the products so you can see the best sellers and determine which ones are popular. Look for common threads among them—and, more important, the gaps you could fill.

TRADE JOURNALS

The intense focus that industry publications bring to a specific field will help you stay aware of the current challenges that industry players may be facing, help you find the resources you need to realize your vision, and introduce you to services and suppliers who will be important to your success. Read several publications in your industry on a regular basis so you can stay in front of what's going on, instead of operating in reactive mode.

TRADE ORGANIZATIONS

Joining an industry group and attending its meetings can be a good way to get candid information on what is going on in a field you would like to enter. You'll be surprised at how many groups there are; ask others who run businesses which ones they find helpful.

Also check out private communities for businesses with a particular interest. Some of these are hyper-focused on offering practical advice to very specific audiences. For instance, eCommerceFuel, a private community for independent e-commerce store owners, targets those with six- and seven-figure revenue. While joining these communities usually isn't free and sometimes requires a substantial investment, the better ones will more than pay for themselves in actionable insights you can use to increase your revenue and profits.

MARKET RESEARCH REPORTS

These compilations, usually written by analysts who study an industry, can be pricey. However, if you are serious about entering a field, they will help you gain a deeper understanding of market forces and the long-term outlook than reading occasional articles will. I have found reports by IBISWorld and Euromonitor, which cover a wide range of industries, to be well produced, but there are many other niche consultancies that offer their own reports. Look for the names of analyst firms that are often quoted in trade journals for clues to which ones are the most credible.

ON-THE-GROUND RESEARCH

Sometimes, there may be very little market research available on the type of product or service you plan to sell because it is too new. In that case you may have to gather data yourself. In a content-related business, this is relatively easy. You can publish information related to what you plan to sell and then gather data on how your audience responds. In a product-oriented business, you may have to survey your customers in the places where they hang out, whether that is on social media sites or at actual brick-and-mortar stores they frequent. This takes some time and effort, but the good news is that if you have to go to these lengths you've probably come up with an idea that is very original and unexplored.

TAKING STOCK

Starting a business can be exciting, but it also requires a lot of energy. By avoiding burnout and refueling yourself with inspiration through the ideas you read about in this book, you can keep that energy flowing. Sometimes, though, it helps to step back completely and think about your big-picture vision and goals and what you really want. To help you pause and reflect, ponder these questions and write down your responses.

What do I truly want from this business?

How do I feel about the day-to-day realities of running it?

Do I want to grow the business or keep it the same size?

Am I comfortable with the amount of time the business leaves me for my relationships and personal interests?

Can I grow the business in a way that lets me keep living my lifestyle—or am I willing to change my lifestyle for a while in order to expand it?

Do I need to hack the way I'm running the business, so it keeps running smoothly as it grows?

Will I ever want to sell this business, or is this something I can see myself doing for the indefinite future?

How does my ultimate goal for the business influence the way in which I need to get things done?

The goal here is to know where you stand, so you can consciously make decisions that support your vision and goals. When you have recorded your responses, try writing a short paragraph about your vision and your number-one goal for the year. You will be surprised by how much having clarity helps you to grow your business in a way that makes you happy.

SHOULD YOU SELL?

Even if you build a million-dollar, one-person business, you may not want to run it forever. So how do you know if it's time to let go and move on to the next thing? I asked internet business broker David Fairley to weigh in.

How do you know when and if to sell a business?

Fairley: There are some practical reasons as well as personal ones. From a practical standpoint, the business may be at least a few years old. Maybe it's reached a plateau and is starting to mature a bit.

It comes down to if the owner or entrepreneur is starting to lose their excitement or passion and starting to get interested in other things.

A lot of people start losing their passion and stop putting in their time and energy. They hit the top of the bell curve and start to sell when it's going down. That's not the time to sell—when your business is showing decreasing revenues or profitability. It's better to recognize when you are losing interest in the business and start thinking then about selling it.

Some people get to the point where growing a business requires hiring more employees, or maybe someone with more experience to whom they have to delegate some leadership. They don't want to take the step of hiring someone and taking on that responsibility. They would prefer to recognize they don't have the skill or energy to take the next step.

How should an entrepreneur prepare a business to sell it?

Fairley: Fundamentally it's about keeping good books you can verify. Have your accountant work with you. Most people who come to sell have QuickBooks set up. It creates more transparency and trust in buyers. Also, it's a good idea to gather your data—your traffic statistics and customer data.

Sometimes, it's like you're going to put a fresh coat of paint on a house. Update the look and feel of your website. These days it's pretty easy to hire someone to do new graphics or create a new template for your site.

Run the business like you don't plan on selling it. Keep thinking: "How can I maximize my customer loyalty and returns? How can I sell more?" That creates more value for the buyer and ensures sales are going to stay stable and grow. That's going to get you a bigger multiple.

What is the best way to handle a sale?

Fairley: There are some people who can sell a business by themselves. But I think like anything you cherish, unless you are really experienced, it may not be a good idea to represent yourself. You are going in kind of blind. A broker offers insights and protocols that are time tested and create security for the buyer and seller. To someone selling a business worth $500,000 or $5 million, it's worth paying a professional to help them prepare the prospectus and documents people need. Another thing a broker is skilled at is putting together a ten- or fifteen-page offering memorandum. That takes a lot of work, and you need to know what to present to get the best offer.

How much does a business broker charge?

Fairley: It depends on the size of the deal. For most businesses in the six figures, it's going to be about 10% [of the gross selling price]. When you get into the seven figures, maybe 8%. I would say for most businesses, it ranges from 8 to 12% depending on who you're working with.

MAKING IT HAPPEN AT A GLANCE

How to Fund the Business

Master the side hustle.

Keep your day job, live lean, and save.

Get others to invest.

Experiment and Revise

Ask your target customer—and listen.

Evolve the product presentation.

Price right for perceived value.

Know when to contract for production,
fulfillment and delivery.

Amplify What Works

Take advantage of social advertising.

Use a major online retailer.

Pick the right social media platform(s).

Build relationships with social media influencers.

Create visual social media.

Build a Steady Income

Hire an accountant.

Realize the power of cash flow.

Use digital marketing to drive daily sales.

Choose either high-volume sales
or premium prices.

Put the Right Systems in Place for Growth

Build media and consumer reviews.

Remove barriers to buying.

Make sales part of customer service.

Invest in public relations and digital marketing.

Review and Reset!

USEFUL RESOURCES

Even if you're super-efficient, it can be hard to get everything done in a one-person business. To help you amp up your personal productivity, I asked the owners of the million-dollar businesses I've profiled in this book to share some of the tools and hacks they use to automate their work and extend their reach, and included some of my own favorites:

ACCOUNTING AND PAYROLL

FreshBooks (freshbooks.com): This entry-level accounting software is aimed at creative types who aren't comfortable with finances but need to keep good records. You can accept ACH payments and credit cards by checking off those options on your invoices.

Gusto (gusto.com): Formerly known as Zen Payroll, this site offers services to help small employers set up payroll, pay contractors, obtain worker's compensation insurance, and provide health benefits.

QuickBooks (quickbooks.com): Accountants often recommend this software, which offers many bells and whistles that you won't find on simpler accounting programs and is useful if you scale to the point where you add payroll.

COMMUNICATION

Globafy (globafy.com): Use this to set up a free conference bridge in many countries around the world, so all participants can each dial in from the country where they are located.

GoToMeeting (gotomeeting.com): If you need high-definition videoconferencing and recorded, high-quality conference lines, this paid service may be helpful.

99designs (99designs.com): Find a designer to help you with projects such as a logo, website, package design and more on this site. 99designs holds design contests in which designers compete to create the best design for you.

Skype (skype.com): This free app allows you to make calls around the world at no charge.

WhatsApp (whatsapp.com): This messaging platform allows you to send instant messages on a mobile platform without paying for SMS.

COMMUNITY

The Brotherhood (brotherhood.net): A selective, by-application-only online support network for entrepreneurs.

eCommerceFuel (ecommercefuel.com): This private community for owners and managers of high-revenue e-commerce stores offers a forum to exchange ideas with fellow digital entrepreneurs.

MastermindTalks (mastermindtalks.com): A by-application-only event, this gathering is popular among owners of high-revenue businesses.

Startup Weekend (startupweekend.com): If you can't get motivated to take the first step toward starting a business in isolation, try attending one of these events in your region.

Ten to Million (tentomillion.com): Real estate entrepreneur Cory Binsfield offers his insights into investing here.

two12 (two12.io): Limited to sixty-five people, this by-application-only business retreat focuses on providing mentoring and creating the opportunity for participants to exchange ideas with other successful entrepreneurs in an intimate setting.

COWORKING

WeWork (wework.com): If you live in a major city, you should be able to find many local providers of coworking space. Fueled by venture capital, WeWork is one of the biggest providers, offering coworking spaces in major cities around the world. You can find coworking spaces through directories such as Coworker (coworker.com), the Global Workspace Association (globalworkspace.com), and deskmag (deskmag.com).

CUSTOMER RELATIONSHIP MANAGEMENT SOFTWARE

Infusionsoft (infusionsoft.com): This is one of many CRM programs that will help you automate your sales and marketing processes. There are many players in this space, with varying capabilities. The best way to find one that's right for your type of business is to ask others with a similar type of business.

Streak for Gmail (streak.com). This free extension for Google Chrome offers many features that will allow you to manage your sales and customer relationships within Gmail.

FULFILLMENT

iPROMOTEu (ipromoteu.com): This service provides order fulfillment and back-office support for sellers of swag.

MARKET RESEARCH

ClickBank (clickbank.com): This giant content marketplace can be an excellent source of ideas on the type of information-based products you can sell online.

Facebook Audience Insights (facebook.com/business/news/audience-insights): This tool will help you generate a detailed demographic of the uses of a product you sell, based on product-interest keywords. Using this service requires a free Facebook business account.

Google Survey (support.google.com/docs/answer/87809?hl=en): This app will enable you to get valuable feedback from your audience. You can use the tool to survey your users on what they'd like you to offer. Another good alternative is SurveyMonkey (surveymonkey.com).

FUNDING

BizPlanCompetitions (bizplancompetitions.com): Search for entrepreneurship contests, elevator-pitch events, and business plan competitions on this global site.

Indiegogo (Indiegogo.com): One of the biggest donation-based crowdfunding sites, Indiegogo is a popular destination for startups looking to raise funding.

Kickstarter (kickstarter.com): Founded in 2009, this donation-based crowdfunding site has now been a launchpad for many a startup, as well as for a wide variety of creative projects.

Techstars (techstars.com): This business accelerator offers an intensive program designed to help aspiring entrepreneurs launch their business in a weekend.

LEGAL

BizFilings (bizfilings.com): This site will help you form a business entity and keep it in compliance.

LegalZoom (legalzoom.com): If you need help with business formation, corporate filings, protecting your intellectual property, or real estate listing, this site offers services that may be useful to you.

PAYMENTS

Apple Pay (apple.com/apple-pay): This service gives your customers a chance to pay securely through their mobile devices.

Square (square.com): You can process credit card transactions from a smartphone or tablet through Square. Unlike merchant services providers, it requires no monthly commitments.

Williams&Harricks (and.co/williams-harricks): By using this app, you can send customers a demand letter for payments when you have exhausted other options.

TALENT-SOURCING

Freelancer (freelancer.com): This global marketplace will help you find professional talent in areas such as manufacturing, product design, web design, and more.

Kalo (kalohq.com): Formerly known as Lystable, this platform enables companies to onboard freelancers around the world, assign tasks, and pay them easily.

Makers' Row (makersrow.com): Find the help you need to manufacture a product, down to the specific factory, on this fast-growing site.

PeoplePerHour (peopleperhour.com): If you have a self-contained project to complete or need freelance talent, this site is a good place to start to find the people you need. Many freelancers offer "hourlies," or fixed-price offers on work they can start immediately.

TaskRabbit (taskrabbit.com): If you're looking for help with deliveries or need a personal assistant, this site can be a good source.

Upwork (upwork.com): This giant freelance platform is a plentiful source of talent in many disciplines, from accounting to writing.

SHIPPING AND DELIVERY

ShippingEasy (shippingeasy.com): If you'd like to automate your shipping and order processing, this site may be a good place to start.

UberRUSH (rush.uber.com): Run by the ridesharing company Uber, this on-demand delivery service offers speedy deliveries in Chicago, the New York City area, and the San Francisco Bay Area.

Zipcar (zipcar.com): Don't have a car? This car-sharing service, available in many urban areas, allows you to take the steering wheel of a shared car when you need to, without the hassles of owning an automobile.

TIME-SAVERS

Dashlane (dashlane.com): This is one of many sites that help you keep track of your digital passwords. The app, which you can download on your phone or computer, is a browser extension for Safari, Chrome, or Firefox. It retains user names, passwords, and other information you want to keep safe, like credit card numbers.

Evernote (evernote.com): This site lets you take notes, gather articles you find online, and create presentations quickly. "It saves my butt every single day!" says Kelly Lester, founder of EasyLunchboxes.

Figma (figma.com): A design platform that enables solo designers to share their work with others and get real-time feedback and collaboration from the community.

Join.me (join.me): This site enables you to share your screen with business contacts quickly and easily, making it easy to do presentations without travel.

ScheduleOnce (scheduleonce.com). One of my favorite time-saving tools, ScheduleOnce lets you share your public calendar with business contacts so they can easily book appointments with you in the time that you are free. It saves me several hours of emailing back and forth to set up meetings every week.

WEBSITE BUILDERS

Shopify (shopify.com): A number of the million-dollar entrepreneurs I spoke with mentioned using this site to put up their e-commerce stores. Many developers are familiar with it, so if you need help, it should be easy to find.

Squarespace (squarespace.com): If you are looking for an easy-to-use platform offering clean-looking templated designs, this site can get you up and running quickly.

Sumo (sumo.com): This site offers a popular newsletter as well as a suite of free tools you can use to increase traffic to your website.

Weebly (weebly.com): Friendly to beginners who have limited knowledge of technology, this site builder makes it easy to put up a website in a day.

Wordpress (wordpress.com): This free, open-source platform is well-tested favorite, especially among those who like a more hands-on approach to web development. It can be adapted so you can do e-commerce from your site.

SUGGESTED ADDITIONAL READING

If you're going to build a million-dollar, one-person business, you can't read too many inspiring books. Here are some that will energize you and provide practical tools for growth.

Choose Yourself by James Altucher
(Lioncrest Publishing, 2013)

James Altucher, a former hedge fund manager, has built a following among millennials who are disenchanted with an economy where big institutions promise security but are crumbling. His book offers ideas on how to take control of your life, whether through entrepreneurship or a career, instead of handing over the reins to others, so you can achieve wealth, happiness, and health.

Making a Living without a Job (Revised Edition) by Barbara Winter
(Bantam, 2009)

Winter, an early guru for the self-employed, embraces the idea that small is better when it comes to businesses. With the collapse of traditional jobs, she sees the potential for great opportunity for personal expression and joy.

Rework by Jason Fried and David Heinemeier
(Crown Business, 2010)

The authors of this popular book have deliberately kept their software company, formerly 37Signals, small but have achieved big results, releasing well-known products such as Basecamp (now their company name). They debunk widely embraced approaches to business, such as working around the clock to get more done and launching with an exit strategy in mind, and offer a road map to creating a lean business that succeeds.

The End of Jobs by Taylor Pearson
(Lioncrest Publishing, 2015)

As the promise of traditional jobs wanes, Pearson makes a compelling case for pursuing entrepreneurship as a career path.

The 4-Hour Workweek by Tim Ferriss
(Harmony, 2007)

This is an entertaining guide to freeing time for adventure by generating passive income, using internet platforms to outsource, and paring down time-wasting obligations. Many of the entrepreneurs I interviewed for this book found reading it to be life changing.

The $100 Startup by Chris Guillebeau
(Crown Business, 2012)

Guillebeau is a digital nomad who travels around the world, making money without a traditional job. In this book, he offers ideas on how to turn a $100 investment into a business generating $50,000 or more, based on 1,500 micro entrepreneurs he identified.

The Simple Living Guide by Janet Luhrs
(Broadway Books, 1997)

This was one of the first books I read about living in an intentional way, so that your lifestyle reflects what really matters to you. I still find myself flipping back through it. Unlike other simplicity books that are focused on extreme frugality, this is a realistic book about how to create a life you are passionate about without superhuman discipline.

The Third Wave by Alvin Toffler
(Morrow, 1980)

For a fascinating look at how the transformation to the digital economy has created both strife and opportunity in society, check out this eerily prescient and very readable book by the writer and futurist who wrote *Future Shock*.

INDEX